D1329720

ROBERT
COOVER

_____ *A Study of the Short Fiction* ____

Also available in Twayne's Studies in Short Fiction Series

Sherwood Anderson: A Study of the Short Fiction
   by Robert Allen Papinchak

Donald Barthelme: A Study of the Short Fiction
   by Barbara L. Roe

Samuel Beckett: A Study of the Short Fiction
   by Robert Cochran

Jorge Luis Borges: A Study of the Short Fiction
   by Phyllis Lassner

Truman Capote: A Study of the Short Fiction
   by Helen S. Garson

Raymond Carver: A Study of the Short Fiction
   by Ewing Campbell

John Cheever: A Study of the Short Fiction
   by James O'Hara

Andre Dubus: A Study of the Short Fiction
   by Thomas E. Kennedy

Gabriel Garcia Marquez: A Study of the Short Fiction
   by Harley D. Oberhelman

John Gardner: A Study of the Short Fiction
   by Jeff Henderson

William Goyen: A Study of the Short Fiction
   by Reginald Gibbons

Franz Kafka: A Study of the Short Fiction
   by Allen Thiher

Flannery O'Connor: A Study of the Short Fiction
   by Suzanne Morrow Paulson

Grace Paley: A Study of the Short Fiction
   by Neil D. Isaacs

V. S. Pritchett: A Study of the Short Fiction
   by John S. Stinson

J. D. Salinger: A Study of the Short Fiction
   by John Wenke

William Saroyan: A Study of the Short Fiction
   by Edward Halsey Foster

Twayne's Studies in Short Fiction

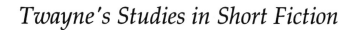

Gordon Weaver, General Editor
Oklahoma State University

ROBERT COOVER. Drawing by Lewis Thompson.

ROBERT COOVER

_____ *A Study of the Short Fiction* ___

Thomas E. Kennedy

TWAYNE PUBLISHERS • *NEW YORK*

Maxwell Macmillan Canada • *Toronto*

Maxwell Macmillan International • *New York Oxford Singapore Sydney*

Twayne's Studies in Short Fiction Series, No. 38

Copyright 1992 by Twayne Publishers

All rights reserved. No part of this book may be reproduced or transmitted in any form or by any means, electronic or mechanical, including photocopying, recording, or by any information storage and retrieval system, without permission in writing from the Publisher.

Twayne Publishers   Maxwell Macmillan Canada, Inc.
Macmillan Publishing Company   1200 Eglinton Avenue East
866 Third Avenue   Suite 200
New York, New York 10022   Don Mills, Ontario M3C 3N1

Macmillan Publishing Company is a part of the Maxwell Communication Group of Companies.

Library of Congress Cataloging-in-Publication Data

Kennedy, Thomas E., 1944–
    Robert Coover: a study of the short fiction / Thomas E. Kennedy.
        p. cm. — (Twayne's studies in short fiction ; no. 38)
    Includes bibliographical references and index.
    ISBN 0-8057-8347-4 (alk. paper)
    1. Coover, Robert—Criticism and interpretation. 2. Short story.
I. Title. II. Series.
PS3553.O633Z75 1992
813'.54—dc20   92-5975
                                                                     CIP

813. 51

C 779 Zk

The paper used in this publication meets the minimum requirements of American National Standard for Information Sciences—Permanence of Paper for Printed Library Materials, ANSI Z39.48-1984.

10 9 8 7 6 5 4 3 2 1

Printed in the United States of America.

For the three of you

Monique, Daniel, Isabel

METHODIST COLLEGE LIBRARY
Fayetteville, N.C.

Contents

Preface   xi
Acknowledgments   xiii

PART 1. THE SHORT FICTION

Introduction   3
Pricksongs & Descants   12
In Bed One Night & Other Brief Encounters   68
A Night at the Movies or, You Must Remember This   73

PART 2. THE WRITER

Introduction   97
Interview, 1979   98
    Larry McCaffery
Interview, 1986   112
    David Applefield
Interview, 1989   119
    Thomas E. Kennedy

PART 3. THE CRITICS

Introduction   127
William H. Gass   128
Joyce Carol Oates   131
Susan Kissel   132
Neil Schmitz   133
Jon Zonderman   134
Charla Gabert   135
Caryn James   139
John O'Brien   140

Chronology   141
Bibliography   145
Index   149

Preface

My objective in this study of the short fictions of Robert Coover is to look as deeply and thoroughly as I can into his most important stories. To the best of my knowledge, such an investigation has not been undertaken before; although his novels have been studied in depth, his short fiction tends to be dealt with as a single chapter of the greater body of his work. My hope is that this book will be useful for teachers and students as well as for the unaffiliated reader, for those seeking an entry to understanding Coover's short fiction as well as for those who wish to compare their own ideas about it with someone else's. I have focused exclusively on his three collections: *Pricksongs & Descants* (1969), *In Bed One Night & Other Brief Encounters* (1983), and *A Night at the Movies or, You Must Remember This* (1987).

In addition, I refer throughout the text to the work of other critics on Coover, most especially Richard Andersen's *Robert Coover* (1981), Jackson I. Cope's *Robert Coover's Fictions* (1986), and Lois Gordon's *Robert Coover: The Universal Fictionmaking Process* (1983). In parts 2 and 3 other critical points of view, pro and con, are presented as well to give the reader the opportunity to compare and contrast.

I have not felt obliged to deal with Coover's uncollected short fiction. Much of it seems to me less powerful—some of it decidedly so—than most of his collected work, and I felt that, in dealing at length with the three collections, I had exhausted what I wanted to say about Mr. Coover's genius for the short form.

Of the three books of stories I have studied, I use more space discussing his brilliant *Pricksongs & Descants*, which is, in my opinion, the most powerful of the three; all three, however, bear the distinct mark of his brilliance as a writer determined to force the reader to confront the "mythic residue" that is the existential terminology from which contemporary society creates its identity. I hasten to add that my high praise of *Pricksongs & Descants* is not intended to denigrate the unique achievement of *A Night at the Movies* in fictionally confronting the great American medium: film.

When, rarely, Mr. Coover is less successful, his work tends toward a kind of bawdy glitter that is not unamusing but seems not to profit from critical analysis. I am thinking most specifically of the uncollected "Lucky Pierre" stories; a couple of examples of this are also found in the collections, so that I have had the opportunity to touch on this aspect of his work in this study. I was once invited by *Playboy* magazine to comment on the latest version of the "Lucky Pierre" stories to appear in print ("Lucky Pierre at the Doctor's Office") and found myself lost for words other than the ribald ("So Lucky Pierre, you restless fucker, we meet again . . . " etc.). I much preferred to spend time dealing with those of his works whose implications, though frequently equally bawdy, seem to me to run deeper and reach further.

Coover at his best is a great innovative writer of short fiction, a brilliant metafictional strategist, a writer with the grasp to perceive and courage to follow a vision of astounding originality, and it is what I consider his best that I wish to take as my main focus here.

Acknowledgments

Appreciation is due to Larry McCaffrey and David Applefield and their publishers for allowing me to reprint portions of their fine interviews with Robert Coover which originally appeared in, respectively, *Anything Can Happen* (Urbana: University of Illinois Press, 1983), and *Frank: An International Journal of Contemporary Writing and Art* (Paris) (1987), and to the following authors and publications for permission to reprint excerpts of their works: William H. Gass (*New York Times*), Joyce Carol Oates (*Southern Review*), Neil Schmitz (*Novel*), Susan Kissel (*Studies in Short Fiction*), Caryn James (*VLS*), John O'Brien (*Washington Post Book World*), Jon Zonderman (*American Book Review*), and Charla Gabert (*Chicago Review*).

It is always a question whether the less demanding critical task is to be the first person to do scholarship on an author or to seek a yet untouched area of an already widely studied author's production from which to work—in my case a focus on Mr. Coover's short fiction. This focus has given me the opportunity to explore at greater length and, I hope, in greater depth than previous critics those Coover stories that I consider his most important and that other critics, who have dealt more with his novels, have not treated as extensively. Nonetheless, there is no doubt that appreciation is also due, and I grant it happily, to those scholars whose engaging book-length studies of the whole body of Coover's work I had the benefit of consulting in the preparation of my own book, particularly Richard Andersen, Lois Gordon, and Jackson Cope, as well as the authors of numerous articles and reviews that were available to me, many of which are referred to in the text. If at times I seem to quibble with these critics, it is not as an opponent so much as in the spirit of excited, friendly conversation about a mutually appreciated subject, and I hope that the authors in question will take it as such.

I would also like to thank Karen Kirk Sorensen and Inge Glud at the Documentation Center of the American Embassy in Copenhagen for their kind help in this and other projects. A word of tribute is due as well to the excellent Danish public library system, which enabled me to obtain books that would otherwise have been unavailable.

Acknowledgments

I owe a great debt to Gordon Weaver, general editor of Twayne's Studies in Short Fiction series, for his indefatigable willingness to read, listen, reread, and advise from his multiply expert vantage points of fiction writer, critic, professor, and editor. I am also greatly indebted to Elizabeth T. Fowler, Twayne house editor of the Series, for her tireless enthusiasm, aid, encouragement, patience, and kindness, as well as to Vida Petronis, India Koopman, and Cindy Buck.

I wish to express my loving thanks to three unofficial consulting editors: my children, Isabel and Daniel, for helping me to explore the instinctual response to the fairy tale that facilitated my coming to terms with the implications of Coover's work in the fairy tale genre; and my wife, Monique Brun Kennedy, whose keen intellect and penetrating insights have been my most important source of inspiration for two decades.

Part 1

THE SHORT FICTION

Introduction

Robert Coover is one of the great innovators of contemporary American fiction. Primarily a novelist, Coover's first collection of short fiction, *Pricksongs & Descants*, published in 1969, had an immediate impact upon the writers and readers of the time.[1] The novellas and two collections he has published since then have all had an influence on the writing and understanding of American short fiction and on American culture.

The short fiction of Robert Coover is an integrated part of the culture in which it appears. It would be difficult, for example, to read *P&D* with full appreciation without knowing something of Grimm fairy tales, the Bible, the TV game show format, American movies and movie houses of the 1940s and 1950s, and the art of fiction as practiced in the United States in the latter half of the twentieth century, the "wreck" of which Coover seeks "to intuit the enormity of."[2]

To satisfactorily appreciate Coover's short fiction in context requires some preliminary consideration of the situation of American fiction of the past three decades and the attitude of publishers, writers, and readers toward realism and reality in American fiction. In the 1960s a curious thing happened in American fiction. Writers divided into two opposing groups: One moved toward what purported to be "real life," and the other engaged itself with reality as artifice, distancing itself from everyday perceptions of reality in order to explore reality's greater dimensions as well as the dimensions of the art that defines reality.

The Real-Life Writers: Subjective Journalism/Objective Fiction

The group of real-life fiction writers merged their craft with that of journalism to produce what was sometimes called subjective journalism, sometimes the nonfiction novel (what might be called "objective fiction.")

Thus, Truman Capote's *In Cold Blood* (1960) presented a fictionalized account of a murder in Kansas that holds closely to the available facts in the case; it was written after several years of research and interviews with the real-life "characters." Norman Mailer, too, began to write what he has called "history as the novel, the novel as history."[3] *The Armies of the Night* (1968) and *Miami and The Siege of Chicago* (1969) contain fictionalized journalistic reports of three of the more devastating political events of the Vietnam era: the 1967 peace march on Washington, D.C., and the Democratic and Republican national conventions to nominate their candidates for president in 1968. Where history and fiction join in these accounts is in the person of the narrator, whose name is Norman Mailer. We are in that way provided with a filter through which to view the events being reported—in contrast to conventional journalism, whose third-person reportage reveals, ideally, no shadow of the reporter informing us. Mailer later imitated Capote's achievement by writing a novel—*The Executioner's Song* (1979)—whose real-life character, Gary Gilmore, was a multiple murderer on death row in Utah fighting not for his life but for his right to be executed.

At the same time, journalists such as Tom Wolfe, Jimmy Breslin, Pete Hamill, and Hunter S. Thompson were writing newspaper reportage and books so clearly subjective that the borders between fiction and reality seemed for a time to evaporate. Tom Wolfe today urges fiction writers to go out into the world and take notes and write "realism," in much the way that Truman Capote years ago belittled the earlier fiction of Norman Mailer by saying that it was all just "made up in his head," implying that using the imagination—communing with the "muse" or collective unconscious, recognized all the way back to Homer as a kind of religious state—suddenly was an asocial, solipsistic act of aesthetic onanism.

The error here seems clear: the real-life fiction writers confused realism with reality, and fiction or art with real life. It was the French novelist Emile Zola who said, "The realists of art ought to be called the illusionists." Realism is a fictional technique whereby the writer seeks to convince the reader that the fictional world he is creating corresponds to the real world where the reader sits, looking in through the window of a book. The successful realist will convince the reader that his New York, for instance, is an impeccable reproduction of the real one, thus co-opting the idea of a real place as a stage upon which to set his actors in motion, as Tom Wolfe attempts to do in *Bonfire of the Vanities* (1988). Similarly, the realist seeks to convince the reader that his characters are persons, made of flesh and blood, although in fact, as the writer-philosopher William H. Gass points out in his brilliant book of fictional theory *Fiction and the Figures of Life* (1970), they are nothing but words. He compares this discovery to being as shocking as if one suddenly were "to discover that one's wife were made of rubber."[4] The point is that realism is a fictional technique whereby a writer creates an illusion of reality with words.

Illusions as Doors to the Greater Reality

While Capote, Mailer, Wolfe, Breslin, and others were busy trying to find reality by merging subjective journalism and objective fiction, another group of American writers were moving in an opposite direction, seeking reality not via realism but via more blatant illusions, seeking a reality not limited to the mundane daily movements of our lives so much as a panorama of our powers of spirit, language, perception, and existential freedom. More important, they explored illusions that go beyond the scope of the weary fictional conventions that present the linear movements of realistic characters through a complication-climax-resolution of "plot." The realism that was passing for reality had grown stylized. It is interesting to think that the experiments of painting had been so readily incorporated into the reality perceptions of the Western world that few sophisticated people would be caught dead hanging a representational picture on their walls. But those same people might continue to prefer "representational" (realistic) fiction.

Among the writers who departed from conventional realism were three of the great American innovators of the period: John Barth, Donald Barthelme, and Robert Coover. Even Bernard Malamud, often a realistic writer, turned in this direction with works such as his marvelous story "The Jewbird" (1963) and the novel *Pictures of Fidelman* (1969). Many other writers were also experimenting, but Barth, Barthelme, and Coover are among the very best. Their best nonrealistic works include Barth's *Lost in the Funhouse* (1968), Barthelme's *Unspeakable Practices, Unnatural Acts* (1968), and Coover's wonderful *Pricksongs & Descants* (1969). Perhaps more than any others in the United States, these three writers shifted the focus in American fiction, for a time, from content to process, and to the existential significance of the process of fiction for the creation of human identity: we are all, metafiction seems to say, our own fictions, created by ourselves of our perceptions and the language with which we express them.

The "Victory" of Realism

These writers are well known but perhaps are not better known because the "fight" between the two camps of American fiction in the 1960s and through the 1970s was "won" by the realists. Early in the 1980s the British magazine *Granta* proclaimed the "new fiction" in America to be "Dirty Realism," also known as minimalism, neorealism, and K-mart realism.[5] Writers like Raymond Carver, Frederick Barthelme (the realistic younger brother of the innovative Donald), Bobbie Anne Mason, Andre Dubus, and Tobias Wolfe reign in this domain.

Shortly before his death, Raymond Carver said in a 1987 interview in the Paris-based American literary journal *Frank:* "The work of many of the writers who came into prominence in the Sixties is not going to last. . . . Literature is coming back to the things that count. . . . Readers have gotten tired of fiction that's gotten too far away from the real concerns."[6] Carver was a splendid writer. Therefore, it is surprising to find that he apparently failed to understand or appreciate the fictional innovations of the 1960s and 1970s. As we enter the 1990s, we find ourselves in the United States in a period of great literary wealth: writers of all persuasions—realists, postmodernists, metafictionists, surrealists, fabulists—are at work. Yet *Colorado Review* recently suggested that there seems to be a desire at large to make realism into a kind of "State Fiction" in the United States.[7] Even Thomas Pynchon's most recent novel, *Vineland* (1990), moves toward realism.

This sudden revision from innovation to realism, or neorealism, would seem to be a reflection of the consumer philosophy, the throwaway aesthetic: use it up and throw it away; get rid of the old, bring in the new. The key word in such an approach to fiction is *new.* What is now new (and therefore worthy of our praise)? What is now old (and therefore no longer deserving of our admiration)? The word *modern,* from the Latin for "just now," once seemed to imply an art of constant renewal, of continuing process. The term is used by some English-speaking critics to suggest a period that is past—it is associated with names of dead writers, James Joyce, Samuel Beckett, Franz Kafka—and has now been displaced by odd, already aging terms like "postmodern" and "postcontemporary" and "metafiction," 1980s terms used to describe a fiction that in the 1960s and 1970s was, itself, introduced as "The New Fiction." Now, apparently, that "new" fiction has grown old, and the *new* new fiction, in the words of the editor of *Granta,* makes "postmodernism" seem "pretentious" and modernism "false" (Bufford, 4-5)—in other words, the old new fiction, once hailed as the ultimate existential statement, is now seen to have been a mere pose, a pretense, a flashy mask with no face behind it, *wrong.*

As the late Donald Barthelme's fictional critic Alphonse puts it: "Postmodern is dead. A stunning blow, but not entirely surprising. . . . What shall we call the New Thing . . . which is bound to be out there somewhere? Post-postmodernism sounds, to me, a little lumpy. . . . It should have the word *new* in it somewhere. The New Newness? Or maybe the Post-New?"[8]

In truth, the beauty of art is that it is in continuous expansion. Every work of art has a potential for immortality. Art is not a soup can that we empty and throw away. And the fiction of all ages is still with us and vital. If we ask the neorealists to name the greatest of their masters, as likely as not they reply, Chekhov.

Coover, the Innovator

Innovation (from the Latin *in* + *novare*, or *novus*, new) is another term which indicates renewal in fiction, finding new approaches to fiction's tasks of entertaining and enlightening us. It is, of course, questionable whether anything is really new in fiction. If we read a story like Nikolay Gogol's "The Nose" (1836), we might wonder if postmodernism in fiction was born 150 years ago in Russia.

Nonetheless, readers and writers belong to a time, and our innovators serve us by refreshing our sense of what literature is, what it does, what it can do *now*. Innovators confuse us to save us from faulty, conventional understanding. Similarly, such a writer might take the worn out illusions of the realist and destroy them before the reader's eyes only to create an even stronger illusion. Coover performs this feat repeatedly in his short fictions, in ever surprising ways: by applying the techniques of contemporary realism to the Bible or the fairy tale, by discussing the structure in which his fictional characters are created, by creating them before our eyes, and by musing over their seeming "concreteness."

Some of the extraordinary pieces in Coover's first collection, *Pricksongs & Descants*, have been widely anthologized and studied in university fiction courses for the power of their vision and their undoing of the traditionally accepted gambits of short fiction, with its prevailing emphasis on realism, sociology, linearity, and mimesis. Coover's fiction presents a comic nightmare that stimulates at one and the same time dark visions and belly laughs, reuniting high and low, brain and gut. His imaginings of human existence lie on the far side of the looking glass. There, vulgarity occupies a place of honor to the right of the sublime, and his play with realistic technique, via repetition, variation, parody, and exaggeration, achieves cosmic visions of great power and depth not readily accessible to more conventional realistic fiction.

Coover's greatest work is probably the big novel *The Public Burning* (1977), which is "based on" the political career of Richard M. Nixon, although it can hardly be equated with the subjective journalism/objective fiction discussed earlier. Still, I believe his most powerful work is *Pricksongs & Descants*, a book of wonders.

P&D combines the real and the surreal in much the same way that fairy tales do. As the late Bruno Bettelheim described it in *The Uses of Enchantment* (1968), fairy tales "usually start out in a quite realistic way: a mother telling her daughter to go all by herself to visit grandmother . . . "; but what follows is a series of increasingly mythical, symbolic, often terrifying occurrences.[9] Bettelheim was not speaking about Coover, but the comparison is apropos. In fact, among the many kinds of fiction presented in *Pricksongs & Descants* are postmodern retellings of the Grimm fairy tales ("The Door" and "The Gingerbread House"), a number of tales more or less clearly taken from the Bible ("J's Marriage," "The Brother"), and other stories unlike anything seen before or since (except in rank imitation).

To many of us, life sometimes seems little more than a series of repetitions of meaningless events: we rise, we eat, we go to work, we come home again, we eat, we look at the television, we sleep, rise again, eat, and so on. Coover's "The Elevator" may be looked upon as a realistic rendering of such a life, perhaps more realistic than surrealistic, although in fact it is a classic piece of metafiction. The story hangs in the mind because it achieves the kind of emotional-intellectual coherence that can be brought forth via the deliberate violation of the traditional expectations of coherence or meaning that so much mainstream fiction, even by highly respectable writers, has handled to a flimsy thinness. We all know these types of stories: heartbreaking tales of divorce, descent into alcoholism, corporate struggle in which the little man pits himself against the evil establishment, metaphorical tales of the little man pitting himself against nature, other men, himself, and so on. Some of them are good, too. John Updike breaks your heart telling the sad story of his *Couples* (1968) losing their connection with one another and splitting apart and never really knowing what happened. But as Lawrence Millman has observed, fiction must have more to talk about than divorce, mixed drinks, and furniture.[10]

Coover's work is a complex alternative for those who prefer the pleasures of the difficult lodged in the delight and befuddlement of a reality far greater than mere realism or "fictional therapy." A story like "The Babysitter," for example, collages a multitude of reality's possibilities in a comic parody that functions on myriad levels. If one is expecting dramatic structure of the mainstream realistic story, or even the deep as well as surface coherence of Ernest Hemingway, William Faulkner, or F. Scott Fitzgerald, Coover's work might seem baffling.

It is difficult to come to critical terms with stories of such power. Why? because, I think, they have no simple meanings. Coover's stories are multi-formed vehicles of "reality" that encompass varying "realities" and literary genres—fantasy, myth, love story, soap opera, slapstick comedy, parable, myth, daydream, or nightmare. A Coover story functions much like a cubist painting: presenting myriad points of view at once and showing us finally that reality is *not* fixed, as conventional literature would have it, that it is *not* a single, linear event, based on cause and effect, that leads through complication to climax and resolution.

These are the themes and subjects of Coover's short fiction: he deals with life, life viewed through the lens of art, as well as the process of that viewing and the process of his own fictional handling of it all. He uses techniques of realism to turn classic tales into metafictions that deliver the reader to a new level of reality. He takes the reader out of the narrow confines of fictional realism, expanding the walls of the house of fiction to contain vastly greater aspects of the reality in which we live.

It is perhaps a commonplace to compare the 1980s with the 1950s in America, and an inaccurate commonplace at that. Much of what happened in the 1960s and 1970s acts as a wedge against our return to a time so laced with restrictions that a naked human body could evoke legal action, a Supreme Court decision was required to legislate the free movement of people with dark skin, and writers were prohibited by law and convention from using certain words of the English language. (Or do we, in fact, see a number of these restrictions reemerging in the United States of the 1990s?) Yet the spirit of innovation in fiction that emerged from such restraint, reaching always toward and beyond the border of "conventional" reality, seemed in the 1980s to have provoked a "realistic" backlash not unlike the homespun "self-evident" realities of the 1950s. This backlash echoed, for instance, in Carver's preference for "the things that count" and "the real concerns"—by which I suppose he meant "reality."

But all art, all serious art, deals by definition with the reality of human existence and attempts to touch that reality or some part of it. Realism works on sociological premises with a more or less conventional reality—the conventions by which, for example, in our daily lives we tacitly agree to ignore whatever in ourselves is not congruous with daily "sane" behavior, with an orderly, ordered view of the world. In other words, to achieve a semblance of order we pretend that the conditions of life are reasonable and just, we edit our mad dreams and desires and all that is extraneous to the convention of order. We pretend to believe that *Time* and *Newsweek* and *The Economist,* and even the *New York Post* and the *Daily News* and (literalist of the postmodern imagination) the *National Enquirer,* are capable of reporting what we need to know to understand our world, and that "realistic" fiction can reflect a coherent picture of a coherent world.

Coover seeks to more fully embrace reality, both "raw" (human behavior) and "processed" (fiction, film, TV). The realities he serves us can be dark, absurd, frightening—even as they make us laugh with nervous glee—or they can be hauntingly beautiful. The innovation and invention of a Coover are required to portray reality in the fullness of its tension and contradiction. Realism alone cannot manage the whole job before us of coming to terms with these mad times in this strange condition of existence.

The work of the great American innovators in fiction that began to emerge in the 1960s remains fresh and important to the continuing work of fiction as a means of expression for the spirit of a country still seeking an identity beyond that of sociopolitical cliché. The innovative style of writers like Coover provides a vital alternative to the predominant schools of realism and sociological fiction. Clearly, the work of the innovators is not yet done. The powerful vision presented in Coover's short fiction continues to delight and enlighten, to elucidate the experience of existence in the Western world and, specifically, in the United States toward the end of the twentieth century. The short fictions of *Pricksongs & Descants* and *A Night at the Movies* (1988), his two most important collections, represent the contemporary American story at its highest level.[11]

It is marvelous now, more than 20 years after the appearance of *Pricksongs & Descants,* to consider the eagerness with which the American imagination welcomed Coover. It is perhaps even more marvelous to consider that Coover's work has never been *assimilated* into the mainstream of our culture. It has survived and has without doubt influenced the work of other writers and the culture in general, in the way that art of great power will cause a stir that reaches even those who know nothing of its existence. (Could the metafiction of Paul Auster's *New York Trilogy,* for example, ever have achieved such popularity if Coover had not prepared the American consciousness for them?) Coover's work has, in fact, elicited violent attempts to eject it from that culture—evidenced most recently in brick-throwing attacks by ideologues upon bookshops carrying a reprint of Coover's novella *Spanking the Maid* (1982), another example of a literalist failure of the imagination necessary to an appreciation of Coover's achievement.

Thus, today's reader discovering Coover's short fiction for the first time is as shocked, baffled, delighted, infuriated, and enlightened as the reader of the 1960s. The innovative forces at play in American fiction of the 1960s and 1970s will indeed survive and will keep us from getting lost in the narrow fictions that out of habit and weariness take the place of the greater reality in which we are adrift, our only tool of navigation the imagination.

The short fiction of Robert Coover represents only a small part of his opus: only two of seven full-length books and a number of slimmer volumes, many of which have been incorporated into other, longer works. Some might argue that his greatest achievements are the novels, *The Origin of the Brunists* (1966), *The Universal Baseball Association Inc., J. Henry Waugh, Prop.* (1968), *The Public Burning* (1977), *Gerald's Party* (1986), and the recent *Pinocchio* (1991), yet few knowledgeable critics of American fiction would attempt to discount the extraordinary power and significance of Coover's short fiction.

This book, then, is a tour through the universe of that short fiction to examine, discuss, and admire its power.

Pricksongs & Descants

"The Door: A Prologue of Sorts"

We enter the world of Robert Coover's *Pricksongs & Descants* first through the comic double entendres of its title, next through the comic juxtaposition of the bawdy *Fanny Hill* and elevated Paul Valery epigraphs, and then through a door—or rather, a six-page approach to a door whose threshold we merely cross before the door latches firmly behind us (*P&D*, 19)—into a place where all is determined by the power of imagination, our own and the imagination of those who came before us. There begins Coover's imaginative examination of those realities previously imagined for us. And to navigate this place, the reader must not only think and feel but, most important, *imagine*.

"The Door" presages the Cooverian feats to come in *P&D*. In six pages, three points of view obliquely interweave three fairy tales known to virtually every American and European reader, tales that have been told and retold, parodied, farced, emasculated, prettified, mocked, and made endearing by everyone from Charles Perrault in seventeenth-century France to the Brothers Grimm in nineteenth-century Germany to Walt Disney in twentieth-century Hollywood, in every media from print to film, plays, and cartoons, from glittery picture books to the somber mud-colored volumes of serious childhoods: "Jack and the Beanstalk," "Beauty and the Beast," and "Little Red Riding Hood." Snippets and hints of other tales indicate that this prologue is a universe of fairy tale not unlike the eerie "Toon Town" of Steven Spielberg's recent *Who Killed Roger Rabbit?* (1989).

The tale told in these six pages is, as with most of Coover's work, multi-layered. He plays with a surface realism of tone at once comic and convincing—a hallmark of Coover's power. We chuckle at his brooding Jack, turned giant in the woods, begrudgingly playing his part in the tale at the same time as we accept him as a psychologically "real" character in a way impossible with the classic fairy tale form, wherein misty omniscience of narration distances us from all the characters and events.

Similarly, the bawdy grandma's internal monologue becomes a comic-convincing mix of the Wife of Bath, Molly Bloom, and Ma Kettle, a grumbling old woman awaiting her due, the "goodies" of Red Riding Hood's basket, while she mutters with grudging affection over the beast whose "doggy stink" she has "suffered a lifetime of ... and still no Prince, no Prince ... " (*P&D*, 17).

Red Riding Hood herself is a willing victim in this ritual of innocence; she drops her cloak and enters the open door, closing it fast behind her. The wolf is nowhere in sight. We know him only through the references in grandma's monologue to "his old death-cunt-and-prick songs" (in case anyone was in doubt about the pun inherent in the book's title). This is an interesting twist, particularly given the erotic directness of Coover's version of the tale, since the wolf is the story's powerful core of reality. In his *The Uses of Enchantment* Bettelheim quotes Djuna Barnes from *Nightwood* (1936): "Children know something they can't tell; they like Red Riding Hood and the wolf in bed!" (176).

Bettelheim further explores the early Perrault "moral fiction" version of the story in which the wolf lies naked in the grandmother's bed and has the girl undress and join him, replying to the girl's observation on the size of his arms, "All the better to embrace you!" The Perrault tale fails, however, because its conclusion is explicitly moralistic, perverting the function of the fairy tale, the natural role of which is to express a *"rite de passage*—such as a metaphoric death of an old, inadequate self in order to be reborn on a higher plane of existence" (Bettelheim, 35).

Clearly, this function is also at the heart of Coover's "Door." Neil Schmitz's complaint that Coover's versions of the tales are "little more than adulterated versions of the TV cartoons" seems stuck at the superficial level of style, the disgruntlement of a highbrow who is so stuck among the groundlings at the Globe Theatre that he is unable to catch the deeper nuances.[1] Coover can so adeptly combine slapstick and farce with more profound existential portrayals that he can in fact draw the one from the other, can identify their common ground.

"The Door" is a retelling of the fairy tales that is at once parodic and comic, psychologically realistic, generally metafictional (a fiction about fairy tales and their existential meaning), and specifically metafictional (a preparation for the world of the book the reader is entering). The piece yields further facets: in addition to being a tale of rite of passage from innocence to maturity—with its parallel metaphor of rite of passage for the reader from a conventional to an innovative reading of fairy tale, from conventional to innovative fiction, and from fiction to metafiction ("Jack the myth killer has become Jack the mythologizing narrator whose false narrative the girl leaves behind for a new reality."²—it is a story of generational cycles, again, on both the human and literary levels.

Coover's Jack, who has slain his giant (the fairy tale equivalent of the child becoming a man, the child slaying his dependence on parents), is now his own giant and the father of Riding Hood. He has taught her to love life, but in his tales of gaiety, out of "his cowardly lonely love, he'd left out the terror" (*P&D*, 14). He berates himself for having done this—leaving the girl vulnerable to her ignorance of life—and fears that she will end up hating him for it. At the same time he resents his own mother (grandma!), who, like all women, "went birthing hopelessly sentient creatures into the inexplicable emptiness, giving carelessly of their bellies, teats . . . into addled uselessness, humming the old songs, the old lies" (*P&D*, 14–15)—again, the challenge to convention.

It is interesting that the father in this fairy tale has denied his daughter knowledge of a terror we will later learn she already has some sense of. "He's pretended to her that there were no monsters, no wolves, or witches, but yes, goddamn it, there were" (*P&D*, 15). Coover employs a shrewd strategy here by omitting direct reference to the wolf, paralleling not only Jack's strategy but that of "many intelligent, well-meaning, modern, middle class parents," who deprive their children of fairy tales because, inter alia, they are too harsh or too untruthful (Bettelheim, 24). Coover's Jack seems to presume that it is the knowledge he denied the girl that propels her toward that very thing he has tried, for reasons of love and selfishness, to save her from knowing.

But we move then to grandma's point of view and find an unsentimental, bawdy old bird who scoffs at her granddaughter's naïveté and reminisces about her own earlier "wishful way of neckin ducks and kissin toads and lizards." Grandma is waiting for the girl and knows why she is late, knows that the still unnamed wolf has "got her giddy ear with his old death-cunt-and-prick songs . . . croonin his sacral entertainments." The girl has protested that times have changed, but grandma knows the child is in the spell of her own rising saps ("fuzz on her pubes and juice in the little bubbies" [*P&D*, 16]). Grandma recalls the woes and pleasures of her own life and awaits the child not only for the goodies but also because she has "veils to lift and tales to tell" to the girl (*P&D*, 17).

Finally, we have the Red Riding Hood point of view. From the moment she approaches the cottage she finds that, for the first time in all the years, "the door is open!" (*P&D*, 17). Suddenly, everything seems different to her; the garden itself seems "to speak of a stranger, unimagined garden." She has a sense of all that lay before her *before* she steps across the threshold

("An elaborate game, embellished with masks and poetry. . . . And why not?" [*P&D*, 18]) and "realized that though this was a comedy from which, once entered, you never returned, it nevertheless possessed its own astonishments and conjurings, its towers and closets and even more pathways, more gardens, and more doors" (*P&D*, 18–19).

She steps across, sheds her cloak, and closes the door firmly behind her. Thus, in six pages, Coover begins a marvelous series of prestidigitations functioning on a series of levels, promising the reader the baffling, comic, and enlightening journey into the heart of the imagination that is metafiction. As Bettelheim says, "The 'truth' of fairy stories is the truth of our imagination" (155). So, too, is the truth of the games Coover plays with fairy tale and other forms, the truth of imagination as the faculty with which we invent human reality. And that reality is at one and the same time a mere point of view and a collage of viewpoints—a series of possibilities, a series of doors.

"The Magic Poker"

From the elliptical conclusion of "The Door" *P&D* moves elegantly into the opening sentence of the next piece, "The Magic Poker":

"I wander the island, inventing it," the creative or "self-conscious" narrator informs the reader. "I make a sun for it, and trees . . . and cause the water to lap the pebbles of its abandoned shores. This, and more: I deposit shadows and dampness, spin webs, and scatter ruins. Yes: ruins. A mansion and guest cabins and boat houses and docks. . . . All gutted and window-busted and autographed and shat upon" (*P&D*, 20).

In the 54 brief narrative sequences[3] of "The Magic Poker"—which Coover himself has called "the generative idea" of the collection[4]—we are introduced to five main characters: two sisters in a boat who come to the island, the tall man, the caretaker's son, and the creative narrator. In addition, there are three characters in a fantasy fragment of one of the two girls, and various other bit players, often reflections of the main characters, are presented in the four "once upon a time" beginnings later in the story. We also witness creation and destruction, are told pieces of further tales, fantasies, and thoughts, and experience a fictional universe of Cooverian possibilities where "anything can happen" (*P&D*, 20). In the end, though much has seemed to almost happen, we leave the island uncertain that anything "concrete" has taken place, apart from the comic deconstruction of a host of literary conventions. The final line of the piece informs us that "a frog dies, a strange creature has been slain," but it is not quite possible to know the meaning of this information (*P&D*, 45, scene 54). Coover has enchanted us with this amazing fiction, performing literary magic, and he invents for us an enchanted island not unlike Prospero's; it even houses a Caliban, here called "the caretaker's son." But if Prospero's resignation of his magic reflects Shakespeare's farewell to his art, Coover's act here is the opening of the magic show of his career.

The creative narrator quickly moves from the invention of things whole and ruined to active destruction. By scene 6, he "rot[s] the porch, tatter[s] the screen door . . . infest[s] the walls . . . tear[s] out the light switches, gut[s] the mattresses." He smashes windows, rusts pipes, kicks in walls, unhinges doors, and shits on the bathroom floor. "Really," he tells us, "there's nothing to it. In fact, it is a pleasure" (*P&D*, 22).

From this act of creative destruction he moves to a narration of a "history" of the island and its purchase by a wealthy family (*P&D*, 22, scene 7), and by scene 45 (*P&D*, 40) "people" are saying that the island really does exist, leading the creative narrator to look at a map to discover with surprise that it *is* there. But "who invented this map? Well, I must have, surely." And "the people," too (*P&D*, 40).

Thus, we move, are moved, from creation to the creation of ready-made ruin, to active "creative" destruction to the narration or creation of history, the illusion of which is later destroyed by reference to a "real" geography of the island, which geography is at once discredited via its revelation as fictional illusion: The island is *really* on a map. But *I* invented the map.

*Every*thing in this fiction has been invented by the creative narrator, himself invented by Coover. Yet there are limits here, too, reminiscent of William Gass's rhetorical inquiry as to whether a character in fiction has a nose if he has not explicitly been endowed with one by his author. "Characters in fiction are mostly empty canvas. I have known many who have passed through their stories without noses, or heads to hold them; others have lacked bodies altogether, exercised no natural functions, possessed some thoughts, a few emotions, but no psychologies, and apparently made love without the necessary organs. The true principle is direct enough: [a character] has what he's been given; he also *has* what he *hasn't*, just as strongly."[5]

On this island of Coover's, the borders of this concept are reached, explored, and openly discussed. What does a character have and not have? What is a character given and what can he or she be assumed to have by virtue of being a character (that is, a fictional representation of a human being)? Do characters, as E. M. Forster suggests in *Aspects of the Novel* (1927), have a will of their "own" that can take control of the fiction away from the author, or are they, as Vladimir Nabokov suggests (responding to Forster's point), galley slaves who must do as they are told?[6]

"I have brought two sisters to this invented island," Coover's narrator tells us, "and shall, in time, send them home again. I have dressed them and may well choose to undress them. I have given one three marriages, the other none at all, nor is that the end of my beneficence and cruelty. It might even be argued that I have invented their common parents. No. I have not. We have options that may, I admit, seem strangely limited to some" (*P&D*, 25, scene 15).

In scene 21 the narrator begins to question who has created whom (*P&D*, 27) and in scene 36 he questions his authority over the entire creation: "At times I forget that this arrangement is my own invention. I begin to think of the island as somehow real, its objects solid and intractable. . . . I wonder if others might wander here without my knowing it; I wonder if I might die and the teakettle remain. . . . I have brought two girls to this invented island . . . if they have names and griefs, I have provided them. In fact . . . without me they'd have no cunts" (P&D, 33–34). And: "Where does this illusion come from, this sensation of 'hardness' in a blue teakettle or an iron poker?" (*P&D*, 34).

Throughout the 54 sequences runs a strand of such "reality" creation, transformation, destruction, and questioning, an anti-illusionism that eventually fortifies the illusions it exposes, by the very act of the exposure. By scene 10 the creative-destructive narrator, like Shiva, has been hard at work to provide and destroy, bringing in a green piano (one thinks of Wallace Stevens's "Peter Quince at the Clavier": "Just as my fingers on these keys / Make music, so the self-same sounds / On my spirit make a music, too"[7]; and Peter Quince of *A Midsummer-Night's Dream* [act 1, scene 2] might not seem out of place on Coover's island) and immediately pulling out its wires, yellowing its keys, and cracking its paint (*P&D*, 23). (How curious that the piano becomes even more "real" in its destruction.) By scene 24 a new character who has been introduced along the way, "the tall man," stands on the stone parapet of the island's mansion gazing out on the lake and smoking meditatively: "He has been deeply moved by the desolation of this island. And yet, it is only the desolation of artifact, is it not, the ruin of man's civilized arrogance, nature reclaiming her own. Even the willful mutilations: a kind of instinctive response to the futile artifices of imposed order. . . . But such reasoning does not appease him. . . . [H]e puffs vigorously on his pipe and affirms reason, man, order" (*P&D*, 28)

The philosophizing of this caricature of the male lead in a B-movie or romance novel comically defeats itself; the tall man deduces the meaning of the destruction—"an instinctive response to the futile artifices of imposed order"—but opts to reject it in favor of an abstract view of "reason, man, order." Thus, he willfully imposes the order of abstraction upon his understanding, opting for the "futile artifice" of abstraction. This is the classic representation of the slapstick egghead—as one removed from the unimpeachable sense of instinct (when the girl in gold pants kisses the poker, causing the tall man to materialize, he asks how she thought of doing that and she says, "Call it woman's intuition" [*P&D*, 30]). Yet, of course, it is all abstraction, all made, as Gass points out, "of words and words only"; the string-sprung piano, "concretely" as it appears in the mind's eye, is no less a verbal illusion than the tall man's "idea" of "reason, man, order."

Interestingly, seven scenes earlier (scene 21, p. 30), *l'auteur des choses* has already begun to have a difficult time keeping track of and control over his creations: "But where is the caretaker's son?" he asks. "I don't know . . . this is awkward. Didn't I invent him myself? The girls, yes, and the tall man . . . to be sure, he's one of the first of my inventions. But the caretaker's son? To tell the truth, I sometimes wonder if it was not he who invented me" (*P&D*, 27). Another way of interpreting that statement might be that "an instinctive response to the futile artifices of imposed order" (which the caretaker surely represents) invented the creative-destructive narrator to wreak havoc amid this collage of artifices.

At this point, it would seem appropriate to make a distinction between the narrator and the author of "The Magic Poker." Richard Andersen talks about "the island *Coover* has invented," a conception that might be taken to imply that the "I" of the story is Coover himself (97). We are told, however, that the island is invented by the first-person creative narrator, who is a character in the story; the *story* is what Coover has invented (perhaps an artificial distinction, but a useful one). When, later, one of the girls punches out a window with the poker, we do not say that Coover punches out the window with the poker, but that a character invented by him does. The distinction is useful as a means of considering the narrator's speculation that he may have been created by the caretaker's son, rather than vice versa. It is possible to consider that the caretaker (ragged instinct) may have been the "cause" of the "I"; clearly, though, a character in a fiction cannot "invent" a human being (Robert Coover), though it may consist of an invention of human *identity*: that is, the creative narrator's happy destruction of the island's buildings may reflect Robert Coover's pleasure in "punching out" certain outworn literary artifices under the influence of an instinctual reaction that he follows, though not always without question.

Again, in scenes 27 and 28 the caretaker's son nonpluses the narrator by squatting over a teakettle in the gutted kitchen and depositing in it "a love letter": "A love letter! Wait a minute, this is getting out of hand" (*P&D*, 29–30). He refers back to the poker that he invented earlier in the story and that for a time had been the center of action when one of the two girls had chanced upon it, rusted in the tall grass where the narrator "put it."

Via conventional fairy tale strategies, the girl is led to her discovery of the poker when she is forced to choose between two detours around a spider with a red heart on its belly, whose web obstructs the main path (and what a field day of speculative interpretation that image alone might inspire!). "She chooses the sunny side" (*P&D*, 24, scene 13) and finds the poker, following which discovery the fiction gives us four alternative results: (1) she kisses it and poof! it turns into the tall man; (2) disgusted by the *millions* of bugs beneath it, she throws it down; (3) she kisses it and nothing happens, kisses it again and poof! the tall man appears; (4) she kisses it and nothing happens, only a rotten taste enters her mouth.

In scene 29 the creative narrator turns from the shit in the kettle "back to the poker," where two further alternative scenes are given: (1) The girl is enchanted by the tall man's explanation that she has *not* disenchanted him: "There are no disenchantments, merely progressions and styles of possession. To exist is to be spell-bound.'" (*P&D*, 30) (Can this be the same tall man who earlier rejected the instinct to destroy human artifice now professing that all is illusion and spell?); (2) In scene 32 the tall man is enchantee rather than enchanter: "You are enchantingly beautiful, my dear! . . . Wouldn't you like to lie with me here awhile?" (*P&D*, 31). Or does he seek to enchant (that is, seduce) by professing enchantment?

In Coover's world, things that might otherwise be taken as given, such as "manners," often cross wires in a surprising and comic fashion. By the cultural dictates of the fiction of manners, it is unspeakable that the tall man invites the girl in gold pants to lie with him in so direct a manner; in Coover, the unspeakable is answered with hilariously offhand candor: the girl would be delighted to lie with him, "but these pants are an awful bother to remove" (*P&D*, 31). (This exchange constitutes another of the story's metafictional "destructions": it is a direct "poke" at the fiction of manners, another of the "desolated artifices.")

Here we have the further progression of another strand of story that began with the first appearance in scene 5 of the girl "in tight gold pants" (*P&D*, 21). It will be taken up later in a comic presentation of the story titled "The Magic Poker" within the fiction "The Magic Poker," which is told, in four "once upon a time" variations, by a grandmother (again, the fairy tale element), who is apparently *imagined* by the girl in gold pants herself. The last of the four variations (*P&D*, 42, scene 51) is the most developed and comic one: a king promises the hand of his daughter in marriage to anyone who can remove her tight pants.

These gold pants have been a continuing motif in the story: first as an emblem of the one girl's somewhat shallow and limiting fashion-mindedness, in contrast to the more "natural" and capable qualities of her sister, Karen (*P&D*, 21, scene 5); when she crouches to retrieve the poker, her "haunches flex . . . golden" above the grass (*P&D*, 25, scene 16); later, the pants are once again "gleaming golden over the shadowed grass" (*P&D*, 30, scene 29); and finally, "the tight pants which are still golden here in the deep shadows" (*P&D*, 32, scene 33). Then, in scene 36, we find the creative narrator beginning to meld with the caretaker's son (he "discover[s] the shag of hair between his buttocks") and contemplating "tugging the tight gold pants off" (*P&D*, 34). Next, when the girl in gold pants sketches the tall man (further film and romance fiction clichés), she draws his buttocks "bare and shaggy" (*P&D*, 35, scene 38), and in scene 40 (*P&D*, 36) she experiences a sudden illuminating identification of herself with the sun, an identification that is further elaborated in scene 44 when she tries "to explain about herself and the sun, about consuming herself with an outer fire, while harboring an icecold center within" (*P&D*, 39). Scene 51 presents the fourth of the narrations by the grandmother, imagined by the girl in gold pants, about "a beautiful young Princess in tight gold pants, so very tight in fact that no one could remove them from her. . . . The King at last delivered a Proclamation, 'Whosoever shall succeed in pulling my daughter's pants down . . . shall have her for his bride!' " (*P&D*, 42). Since this is perhaps not the most tempting of trophies, the Princess having been married off three times already in previous competitions, the King sweetens the pot by throwing in the magic poker as well. (We have learned earlier that the "real" girl in gold pants herself has three failed marriages behind her.) Through trickery, the caretaker's son, in the story within the story, gets hold of the magic poker whose magical powers cause the gold pants to drop, after which the Princess kisses the magic poker and poof! it turns into a handsome knight, a variation of the tall man, who draws his sword and slays the caretaker's son while the maiden stands "in the puddle of gold pants" (*P&D*, 43). The knight, says the King, has made the Princess a widow. He instructs her to kiss the knight, but the knight begs her not to—apparently because this will turn him back into the poker, an act paralleled in scene 53, where the sister, Karen, turns the tall man back into the poker.

The girls leave the island then, taking the poker along. "It glistens in the sunshine, a handsome souvenir of a beautiful day" (*P&D*, 44, scene 53). In the final sequence, scene 54, the boat retreats across the lake from the island, becomes a blurred speck beneath the lowering sun, while from the viewpoint of the island "a strange creature lies slain, a tanager sings" (*P&D*, 45).

I would agree with Lois Gordon that the reader "becomes spellbound by Coover's linguistic enchantments" in this story, but I do not agree with her suggestion that one "is utterly incapable of touching the story's richness."[8] Probably one cannot "parse" Coover's story as one can the fiction of a linearist—like, say, Frank O'Connor, whose every metaphor and image in his stories of the Irish troubles stand as an equational symbol on the themes of Irish unity and disunity. The structure of Coover's story is more complex than the fiction of sociology. But one can go a long way in speculation over its rich suggestions, its alternative offerings, its repetitions, contradictions, mergings, doings, and undoings. The narrator creates the caretaker's son, is created by the caretaker's son, and merges with the caretaker's son into the creative-destructive life force, the instinct that is claiming the art of fiction back from the realm of rote artifice.

Yet what "strange creature lies slain" on the island in the final sentence? A frog has died—is it that? The real toads of imaginary gardens perhaps? The frogs that princesses are wont to kiss? Or is it the caretaker's son who is slain in the comic fourth-alternative fairy tale related by the grandmother, imagined by the girl in gold pants, herself imagined by the creative narrator, himself imagined by Coover? If the caretaker's son is the slain creature, what does his death do to our theory of him as the destroyer of outworn artifice? Or is the creative narrator the creative destroyer, while the caretaker's son is a mere destroyer, a beast without the "redeeming social qualities" the U.S. Supreme Court once required of fiction with erotic content if it were not to be judged pornographic? ("Lust!" cries the girl in gold pants when she whacks the caretaker's son with the poker to drive him from an orgy of destruction [*P&D*, 38].) Or is the joke on the tall man, who, released from the poker by the gold-panted princess's kiss, slays the caretaker's son (who is, after all, her lawful fiancé, having succeeded in removing her pants), only to be turned back into the poker by another kiss?

And what are we to make of the poker? It is a magic stick, a thing to stir up fire, real and metaphorical, and its phallic symbolism is directly alluded to (unlike the traditional fairy tale's phallic symbolism, which takes the form of rising sticks and miraculously growing stalks). In scene 39, for example, the sister Karen, doing a comic mime for the tall man, identifies herself with the single "unbroken" window remaining in the house; but she then proceeds to break the window with the poker, which turns into the caretaker's son, whom she follows, with obvious intentions, into the woods (*P&D*, 35). Or in the tale within the tale, the poker is the secret to removing the princess's tight gold pants. (The more circuitous traditional fairy tale metaphors would have been to "awaken" the princess or to "make her laugh.") Also, the poker, when kissed, turns into the tall man (at least sometimes), and when the tall man is kissed (at least sometimes) he can be turned back into the poker. What, one might wonder, do the girls have in mind when they bring the poker home with them as a souvenir?

What is the poker? It is a literal instrument and a magic wand, a phallic symbol and a phallus, a prince and a prick, and a pricksong; the girls on the island merrily transform it from the one to the other, both in "fact" and in "fantasy," and finally, it would seem, the one becomes the other. Karen "takes hold" of the tall man (literary parlance for taking hold of his penis) and draws him beneath her skirt, and what she takes out of her skirt again is the poker. This is at once a playful fracturing of the fairy tale motif and an evocation of that very motif on a level of entertainment and imagination for the adult reader. For what Coover does in this story is both comically entertaining and "serious" (as surely as Shakespeare's *Tempest* is comedy). Each thing destroyed, be it an illusion or a literary convention, becomes, by virtue of its destruction, an object of interest of another sort: for example, the green piano that the narrator has provided and gutted before our eyes is "played" by Karen ("Thunk! . . . Thunk! . . . Thunk! . . . ") in a hypnotic counterpoint to the declaiming speeches of her sister, who compares herself to the sun and postulates about the blameworthiness of those who allow wanton destruction to take place without a protest (P&D, 39, scene 47). The caretaker's son, too, plays the green piano, though a nondestroyed version of it that he drives the fantasy grandmother and children away from so that he can play it with his fists. At first he is frightened by the sound produced when he strikes a key, but after quickly becoming excited by the violent music ("BLAM! BLAM!"), he seizes his genitals with one hand and begins ripping out the piano wires with the other, grunting with delight. Then he seizes the poker and begins smashing windows only to be thwarted by the girl in gold pants, who takes the poker from him and "whacks him on the nates" with it, driving him back into the forest "yelping with pain" (*P&D*, 38, scene 42). Here, then, we have the care-taker's son represented much more unequivocally as pure lust in his destructiveness, rather than as the natural instinct that destroys "futile artifice" implied earlier, and this would seem to clarify the identity-merging between narrator and caretaker's son: some of the destructive instinct is creative, some mere destructive lust.

In one of the four once-upon-a-time fairy tales told by the grandmother—apparently imagined by the girl in gold pants (or perhaps *discovered* by the narrator in his own imagination and then placed in the girl's imagination [*P&D*, 34, scene 37])—the sisters "shat in the soundbox of an old green piano. One of them did anyway; the other one couldn't get her pants down" (*P&D*, 41–42, scene 49). Thus, the green piano is employed in a variety of fashions and serves several different functions.

The fixed elements of the "story" include two sisters presented as somewhat opposite. One is fashionable, the other plain; one is thrice divorced, the other never married; one wears pants, the other a dress; one is uneasy with nature, the other easy with it; one shits in the piano, the other cannot get her pants down to do so; one radiates warmth, apparently around a frigid core, the other, who does not seem an erotic focus, makes sexual use of both the men on the island, the tall man and the caretaker's son, themselves the opposites of B-movie suave and throwback bestial. This sister, Karen, is in fact the only character in the story with a name, discounting "the Dahlbergs," who are nothing other than the name of the never-seen wealthy owners of the desolated island. Karen, in fact, enters the island cool, plain, and capable and leaves it no less in charge: she is in possession of the poker that has variously turned into the tall man and into the caretaker's son and back into the poker again; has solved frigidity and undone metaphoric (and perhaps literal) virginity; and has been used as a weapon to route the beast of lust and a tool to drop pants with.

The girls arrive, the girls depart. They are watched by the caretaker's son, by the narrator who creates the island and them, and by the tall man. By the final scene, as their boat disappears across the lake with the poker in it, they continue to be watched from the point of view of the island itself (or of the narrator?), while on the island "a strange creature lies slain, a tanager sings."

What has happened? What is the story? The reader has been witness to a remarkable series of illusions and anti-illusions, assorted fragments of literary convention, a play of ghost characters amid the ruins doing things in and out of context, a joking play of manners couched in outrageously amusing scurrility. The reader has also been introduced to the haunting images, at once archetypical and clichéd, of a man-beast, a wrecked piano, a desolated island mansion, a tall, dark, turtlenecked, pipe-sucking fop, in a play of illusion within illusion within illusion, a play whose characters are a grain of thought in the brain of other characters, who tell stories in which the host character becomes a player. . . . Here, we are very near the woods of Shakespeare's *Midsummer Night* and the island of *The Tempest*—Coover is a young Prospero dazzling us with his virtuosity.

The question remains: what "strange creature lies slain"? Is the strange creature Caliban? Or the imaginary frog in the imaginary garden of the imaginary island? Or is the strange creature the linear, sociological, narrowly realistic fiction that lies stuck full of holes? Is the strange creature the fairy tale genre, which has been rendered faceless and meaningless by generations of disbelieving realists?

And what bird sings as the story's closing note? A tanager is a New World bird of multicolored plumage. Does Coover suggest that the pricksong is a dazzling New World rhapsody on a green, gutted piano, a symphony for fist, finger, and poker that encompasses the fluent transforming gesture of magic?

"Morris in Chains"

Curiously traditional in a sense, "Morris in Chains" is a less complex, more accessible piece than others in the collection, presenting a fairly straightforward, classic American theme: beneath its sophisticated surface it is a story of science against nature, city against country, reason against myth, the "natural man" (or Pan) as a threat to a scientifically organized modern society and vice versa. As such, it deals with more concrete and well-defined, almost sociopolitical issues than the wider ranging, more archetypical and metafictional explorations, such as "The Magic Poker" and "The Elevator."

Like McMurphy in Ken Kesey's *One Flew Over the Cuckoo's Nest* (1962) (with which Coover's story, though more literary and sophisticated, might be compared), Morris is a natural man being pursued by an unnatural woman intent on emasculating and subjugating him, on curing him of his unruly "patterns."

Quite simply, Morris the shepherd, guilty of keeping sheep, is captured and chained by Doris Peloris, M.D., Ph.D., U.D. (presumably Doctor of Urbanology?). The outcome is given at the start and then reconstructed via alternating points of view: that of an unidentified spokesman for the urbanologists writing the report of the incident, and that of Morris himself, whose interior monologue is spoken in a colloquial, rustic language, half American backwoods, half British countryside.

Morris, on the run through the city's park system, knows his days are numbered ("spite of all they'll get us they'll get us." The urbanologists know, too: "No one doubted the eventual outcome, of course: it was merest Morris versus the infallibility of our computers. . . . Data properly gathered and applied must sooner or later worst the wily old cock" (*P&D*, 48).

What then remains to be told? Only the journey itself, the process, the "hunt." When the computations of all data about Morris, reprocessed into mathematical formulations, prove inconclusive, the doctor announces that "the hunt itself must go on." This is dangerous, for it brings the hunters close to "old temptations": "We might yet be thrilled by the glimmer of disembodied eyes burning hot in the dark forest, by the vision of bathing naiads' bared mammaries or of nutbrown torsos with furry thighs, by the one-note calls of hemlock pipes" (*P&D*, 49). But it is necessary "to grub up, once and for all, the contaminated seed of our unfortunate origin." Polly, one of Dr. Peloris's assistants—one of her favorites, in fact—is suspect: "Her mind wanders. . . . Her butt's too plump" (*P&D*, 50).

Cut to Morris on the run, reminiscing over his past sexual exploits and an odd encounter with a mad goosegirl (the vulnerability of desire in the natural man?) when he spies "that there little plumpbodied scout of theirs" (*P&D*, 52).

Cut to the hunters who find Polly deflowered "in a bed of plastic nasturtiums" (*P&D*, 52), causing the hunt to lose a day. But Morris has troubles, too: an insurrection engineered by his prize animal, Rameses, whom Morris has, with great reluctance, eunuched to keep down the sheep population, as their sheer numbers are slowing him down, increasing the danger (*P&D*, 53). Morris foils the plot and makes amends with his beloved Rameses, but by now Doris Peloris is ready to close in and makes use of her complete scientific control of the situation to prepare every aspect of the snare, right down to the weather and mechanical crickets. The urbanologists have deciphered the order of Morris's disorder to predict with certainty where he will camp next "no matter what operations his mind might undertake in order to arrive at what he would tend to think of as a decision. Unless, of course, it includes the foreknowledge that we await him here. And who knows? Perhaps even this knowledge would not suffice to break the power of pattern over mere mind activity" (*P&D*, 55).

And as Morris waits, he does "feel disaster in [his] bones . . . but it seems like it don't really matter somehow" (*P&D*, 56). In his last hours of freedom, he is inspired by the "bawdy crickets" (that is, the mechanical ones activated by Peloris) "to pipe one of the old songs," a curious composition that seems a cross between a Lewis Carroll parody of an old English ballad and one of the Bokononian rhymes of Kurt Vonnegut's *Cat's Cradle* (1963). Since the song occupies nearly a full page of this 14-page story, it merits more than passing attention for its entertainment appeal as seeming nonsense verse. The song consists of a series of humorous contradictions and black-humorous evocations that spoof the exclamations of the pastoral lyric ("How lovely life, sang I, would be / If only we was dead"), the ballads of suicide-murder-tragic love, followed here not by the customary fatal grief so much as by a limerick-type suggestion of necrophilia, and ending with a call to "Consider less than life a dream / And more than death a song" (*P&D*, 57).

Then Peloris descends on the sleeping shepherd; she strips and examines him while her aides exterminate his sheep, who seem to die "with a certain satisfaction" (*P&D*, 58). The examination culminates in the forcible taking of a semen sample, which is smeared and analyzed on the spot. The doctor then offers Morris occupational rehabilitation in a mutton factory, but he declines and is clapped in chains, where he takes to writing poetry and mourning his dead Rameses. In captivity, Morris's earlier "natural" poetry (describing his encounter with the mad goosegirl, he says "and me composin mad poetries in the back of my agitated skull" [*P&D*, 51]) becomes labored; he fumbles with rhyme and despairs that he is "losin the old touch" (*P&D*, 60). The story closes with his exclamation, "It's the motherin insane are free!" (*P&D*, 60).

Doris Peloris has been victorious, though Morris is not yet "reintegrated." He presents "a challenge serious beyond precedent" to the urbanologists and urbaniatrists, but they have not yet abandoned the possibility of his reintegration.

"Morris in Chains" seems a relatively simple, accessible story among Coover's otherwise multifaceted pricksongs. It is a more or less straightforward variation on the classic American theme of the individual versus the cold forces that civilize, a theme that has been handled in novels, films, and folk songs from Twain to Kesey, *A Thousand Clowns* (1965), and *Cool Hand Luke* (1967), from "John Henry" to Bob Dylan's "Story of the Hurricane." And presumably the theme still lives; the poet's legs are still thick with fur, and he still works, within his chains, to consider less life than dreams, less death than songs.

"The Gingerbread House"

An adequate response to Robert Coover's "The Gingerbread House" requires that the reader be familiar with the details and meaning of

"Hansel and Gretel" and be able to call them to mind for reference in the reading of Coover's version.

Fairy tales, perhaps most especially those of Jacob and Wilhelm Grimm, are told in deceptively simple language; they are based on a sophisticated literary structure and deal in symbol and metaphor, with human development, psychology, and relations. Many adults, particularly of more recent generations, are repulsed by these tales and seek to spare their children contact with narrations of child-abandoning parents, wickedly cruel stepmothers, and old crones who eat little boys and girls. Yet children tend to find the tales both exciting and satisfying and, questioned about them, often exhibit a conscious grasp of the underlying themes.

In "Hansel and Gretel," for example, the child reader comprehends that Gretel starts out as a crybaby and ends up self-confident, capable, and wise, and that both children start out dependent on their parents and, thrust out into the world, win their independence through a series of trials and return home, not as mouths to feed but as providers, completing the cycle from child to parent. The parents who "protect" their children from these tales apparently have themselves not apprehended the magical quality of literary symbolism or the meaning of the harsh metaphors employed. They take the tales too literally and thus reject them as too fantastic, unreal, and horrible, just as both father figures in Coover's "The Door" and "The Gingerbread House" conceal terror and truth from their children.

The extent to which young readers grasp these meanings is another question. Bettelheim suggests it would be dangerous to analyze these tales in depth for a child, but his analyses of them are enlightening for an adult. For the casual reader, no doubt, "Hansel and Gretel" is a simple fantastical entertainment with an underlying theme of children passing from the phase of childish dependence to one of independence. They are forced from their home, devise a plan to return that fails, are abandoned deep in the forest, wander, and come upon a beautifully singing, snow-white dove that leads them to a gingerbread house. They begin to eat the house but are imprisoned by the old crone who owns it and plans to fatten and eat them. By cunning and courage, they outwit and kill the crone, fill their pockets with her jewels, cross the river, and return home to their father, who has been grieving over them, having sent them off against his own better judgment at the demand of their stepmother.

To the casual reader, the details may seem arbitrary, a random assembly of fantasy images strung along the thematic progression, but as all who have considered it more deeply know, "Hansel and Gretel" is in fact a well-structured tale mixing psychological realism with metaphors of a fantastic (the gingerbread house), conventional (the dove), and psychological (the child-eating crone) nature.

In Bettelheim's psychoanalytical terms, the tale is about separation anxiety—the child who clings to the parent to avoid separation is forced out cruelly (11)—and the need to overcome primitive orality (15). Because there is not enough food, they are sent out on their own; they try to return but the bread crumbs they have strewn over their path have been eaten by birds. Then they are led by a snow-white dove (a conventional symbol of innocence, purity, the Holy Spirit, and adolescent passage) to the gingerbread house, which, instead of using for shelter they begin to consume, much as the birds ate the bread that should have led them back to safety (Bettelheim, 160). The house, too, is a conventional symbol for the mother's nourishing body, both pre- and postbirth (Bettelheim, 161).

The old crone who lives in the house represents both oral greed and the mother who has weaned the child: "As mother's attentiveness to the child diminishes with weaning and she begins to be involved in her own activities, the child begins to feel that like the witch she has tricked him in creating a world of oral bliss" (Bettelheim, 163). The child who remains in the oral phase, however, will have his identity "eaten" by the overprotective mother. Hansel and Gretel trick and kill the crone of oral greed and acquire the wealth of spirit necessary for independent action. On the return home, they cross the river (another conventional symbol of passage, this river was not there to cross on their journey *into* the forest) on the back of a white duck (in some versions, a swan). To accomplish this passage the children must separate and go across one at a time, another indication of their development as individuals—they realize they must cross alone and dare to. When they come home, they find their stepmother (the "evil" woman who drove them away) has died. Their father is there grieving over their absence, and they now are able to provide for him.

Bettelheim suggests that one of the functions of the fantastic in a fairy tale is precisely to camouflage the fact that it is dealing with the child's psychological reality, thus sparing the child from the unbearable anxiety that might arise from having to deal directly with that "cruel" reality of inevitable "rejection" by the mother. No child is deliberately deserted in a dense wood; thus, this unreal detail masks the underlying similarity with the child reader's situation and enables the child to find comfort and satisfaction in the tale. There are no witches, but it is exciting to pretend there are, especially when the witch mask conceals the mother's face.

Coover takes it for granted that his reader knows and understands the tale that underlies his piece. Many elements of the original tale (the stepmother, the prologue) are omitted from Coover's version, and others are only obliquely suggested (the reason Hansel furtively marks the path behind him with bread crumbs).

Coover's 15-page tale is told in 42 brief numbered scenes (roughly the same wordage as the Grimm version). An old man leads his two children into the forest. The boy furtively marks his path with bread crumbs while the old man stares straight ahead in despair and guilt (*P&D*, 62). The girl knows what the boy is doing and where the old man is taking them ("but it is nothing but a game!" [*P&D*, 64]): they are on their way to the gingerbread house, from which children do not leave (*P&D*, 65).

Meanwhile, the witch, dressed in black rags, flits through the forest, catches a dove, and tears its heart out (*P&D*, 64). The children sing songs of kings and pretty things, flowers, and "a saint who ate his own fleas" (*P&D*, 62). Doves come and eat the boy's bread crumbs. The boy attacks the dove, the girl tries to rescue it, they fight, and she secures it between her legs, where it dies (*P&D*, 66–67). The witch uses the pulsing, bloody heart of the dove as a lure to seduce the old man (*P&D*, 68–69). The old man tells the children stories of the good fairy and of wishes he privately believes can "come to nothing" (*P&D*, 69). The boy is seduced by the witch (*P&D*, 71). The old man strikes him (*P&D*, 72). The children cling to one another, turning from the old man (*P&D*, 72), who, following a path marked by dead doves, returns home, where he sits gloomily with the ruby-nippled good fairy and makes a wish whose power he does not believe in for the welfare of his children (*P&D*, 73–74). The children, meanwhile, find the gingerbread house and begin to consume it, then see the red, heart-shaped, pulsing door and are enchanted by it, even as they hear the flap of black rags behind it (*P&D*, 74).

In Coover's version, all but a small portion of the original tale is trimmed away; it is embellished with a few new details and focuses more on sexuality and passion than on orality. The witch here is a kind of succubus, and the door to her house is described as a heart, a vagina, that is as red as a jewel, hard candy, a poppy, an apple, a strawberry, a bloodstone, and a rose, sweeter than a sugarplum, and more enchanting than a peppermint stick (*P&D*, 75, 72). The door is a reflection of the heart of innocence torn from the dove, a symbol of life and passion, evil and greed.

What, then, does Coover seek to do with his shortened, refocused, open-ended version of this tale? Is he, as Andersen suggests, inviting "the reader to discover previously unconsidered values in a tale he thinks he has out-grown" (84)? Or is he contradicting the order and symmetry ultimately suggested by the fairy tale to depict a world in which the children must enter a house they cannot leave (*P&D*, 65), must make an existential transition from innocence to passion, to a life whose allure is the bloody heart torn from the breast of the pure dove? His fairy tale for adults depicts not the development of children to adulthood as a triumph of cunning and courage, but their being consumed by the passion at the core of their innocence, where goodness is an impotent radiance in the night, where vitality is an ambiguous mix of greed and lust and wishes for goodness are doomed.

Like Red Riding Hood in "The Door," the children here proceed from the forest to the door, and we leave them at the door, apparently about to enter: "It is heart-shaped and blood-stone-red, its burnished surface gleaming in the sunlight. Oh what a thing is that door! Shining like a ruby, like hard cherry candy, and pulsing softly, radiantly. Yes, marvelous! delicious! insuperable! but beyond: what is the sound of black rags flapping?" (*P&D*, 75). This is perhaps but one of the further doors that Red Riding Hood senses are before her after she enters the door that concludes her story (*P&D*, 19).

"The Gingerbread House" is decidedly not a tale designed to "give comfort," as Bettelheim suggests "Hansel and Gretel" does. Nor, in contrast to many of Coover's other pricksongs, is there much that induces laughter here, aside from the humor inherent in the parodic elements and the occasional throwaway line: "the saint who ate his own fleas." In Coover's tale, instead of guiding the children to the place where they must be to proceed with their development, doves eat the bread crumbs that would have guided them out of the forest. When the old man who has led them into the woods to abandon them returns to his home, he follows a trail of dead doves whose dying screeches we have heard periodically throughout the story as the witch seizes them to tear out their hearts. The pulsing dove's heart is the lure with which the witch seduces first the old man (*P&D*, 68), and later the boy (*P&D*, 71). The boy, for his part, attacks the dove eating his bread crumbs. The girl tries to rescue the creature, and the children fight wildly over it. The girl puts it beneath her skirt, between her thighs, to protect it, but it dies there—an inversion of the virgin birth myth.

The tale itself is an inversion: the children's journey into the woods is unexplained; they are left on the threshold of the pulsing, red, heart-shaped door behind which the black rags of the witch can be heard flapping, the birds of salvation die, their hearts ripped out; and the father sits gloomily at home with the ruby-nippled good fairy and uses up a useless wish for his children's well-being.

Both the father in this tale and the father in "The Door" have sought to protect their children from "terror"; from a misguided love or a fear of hurting them, the fathers have excised terror and darkness from the tales they tell, and they have given their children a stilted view of life. Even as he leads them into the darkness of the forest, the old man tells them bedtime tales of the good fairy and of wishes he secretly knows "come to nothing." It is tempting to draw a parallel to those real-life parents who seek to protect their children from the harshness of fairy tales. Does such "protection" abandon children to the gingerbread house and the witch inside it, the pulsing, bloody dove's heart in her palm? Perhaps that is also a way of viewing the tale. On the other hand, the children in both tales sense the challenge that lies before them; the girl in "The Door" even looks forward to it. The boy in "The Gingerbread House" attempts to avoid it, and the girl knows about it but thinks it all a game.

But what is the "terror"? In both "The Door" and "The Gingerbread House" the terror seems to be of sex, of the ambiguity of the sexual act, or perhaps of the doubleness of passion as creation-destruction, pleasure-pain, beauty-ugliness, hatred-love. Yet the beauty is the impotent beauty of the good fairy with her useless wishes, and the love seems merely to inspire blindness to the truth, leaving the ugliness and hatred of the witch to triumph. Or are those only two parts of the witch?

There might also be a suggestion here that the old man has no choice but to deliver his children to the forest, just as, in real life, parents have no choice but to lead children to their development. What parents do not try to soften life's realities for their children, to conceal their own personal terrors and perceptions of the dark side of life? The old man here is seduced by the witch, lured by the dove's heart pulsing in her hand, and thrashes with her in the brambles, but afterward, when his son succumbs to the same temptation, when his flesh is surprised by the witch, the old man strikes the boy. The adults wish to preserve their children's innocence, but the witch will ensure that the children depart from innocence and never return to it.

In fairy tales we are often told that the protagonists, having completed their developmental adventures and rites of passage, live happily to the end of their days. In Coover, the protagonists are delivered to a new sphere of existence, but hardly one of clarity or of simple pleasure or even, it would seem, of dignity. "The Gingerbread House" might be seen as a fairy tale for adults in which innocence is not lost so much as stripped to the bloody, pulsing heart at its core. Here the children's song "of God's care for little ones" (*P&D*, 61) and the butterflies that "decorate the forest spaces"

(*P&D*, 62) are as fake as the coloring book creatures that people a Walt Disney forest, and the girl's instinct to preserve, comfort, and nourish is doomed to failure. Coover's Gretel cannot save Hansel. Coover's children end up in the house with the bloody heart, while their father ends up a broken man making useless wishes and mourning his children.

Yet the conclusion is ambiguous. Just as the father telling tales to the boy and girl "lets the children complete the story with their own wishes, their own dreams" (*P&D*, 69), so too does Coover leave it to the reader to imagine what awaits the children behind the pulsing door. Presumably, they will meet the life of passion, the witch of desire, but if this is the lot of humankind, how then can it be that the father, following the path of dead doves back to his own home, sits in company with the good fairy, wishing still, apparently, that the goodness of wishes might come to something (*P&D*, 74, cf. 69)? But "it's no use, the doves will come again, there are no reasonable wishes" (*P&D*, 75). There is no way out. This story goes on and on, repeating itself infinitely.

"Seven Exemplary Fictions"

"Prologue"
With this "little book within a book" (*P&D*, 79), we seem to begin again; after 75 pages of recrafted fairy tales, we suddenly reach a formal opening, a direct statement of Coover's intentions in the form of an address to Don Miguel de Cervantes Saavedra. Coover tells Cervantes (and the reader) that these seven stories, along with the three "Sentient Lens" fictions (*P&D*, 168–82) "represent about everything I invented up to the commencement of my first novel in 1962 able to bear this later exposure" (*P&D*, 76–77), just as Cervantes' *novelas* were exemplary because they represented the different writing ideas he was working with from the 1580s until 1612 (*P&D*, 76).

Coover goes on to speak of our need for the imagination, which should be "exercised and in good condition" and of the "solemn and pious charge" upon the writer to see to this task (*P&D*, 77).

This is not metafiction but unadulterated theory; we are given a definition of "the dual nature of all good narrative art": the artist's struggle "against the unconscious mythic residue in human life" and the attempt "to synthesize the unsynthesizable" as he or she sallies "forth against adolescent thought-modes and exhausted art forms, and return[s] home with new complexities." This effort Coover likens to Cervantes' "creation of a synthesis between poetic analogy and literal history (not to mention reality and illusion, sanity and madness, the erotic and the ludicrous, the visionary and the scatological) . . . a revolution in narrative fiction" against the abuse of Romantic conventions (*P&D*, 77).

"Narrative fiction . . . became a process of discovery." But "the universe is closing in on us again. Like you, we, too, seem to be standing at the end of one age and on the threshold of another. . . . We, too, have been brought into a blind alley by the critics and analysts." In this situation, the fiction writer's art constitutes. above all, "challenges to the assumptions of a dying age, exemplary adventures of the Poetic Imagination, high-minded journeys toward the New World" (*P&D*, 78). The writer "uses familiar mythic or historical forms to combat the content of those forms and to conduct the reader . . . to the real, away from mystification to clarification, away from magic to maturity, away from mystery to revelation" (*P&D*, 79). "And," Coover concludes, "it is above all to the need for new modes of perception and fictional forms able to encompass them that I . . . address these stories" (*P&D*, 79).

Thus, holding true to his intention to challenge assumptions and traditions, such as that of the linear, Coover "introduces" his book a third of the way through it and does so in the form of an address not to the contemporary reader but to a man who died the same day Shakespeare did, 350 years before. In so doing, Coover looks not forward but back and demonstrates that he is not undertaking something "new" but rather a repetition of a continuingly necessary process of renewal, cauterizing Coleridge's "film of familiarity" from our perceptions and exposing the old illusions to make way for "new modes of perception and fictional forms able to encompass them" (*P&D*, 79).

"Panel Game"

How fitting to Coover's purpose, then, that this "solemn and pious," high-sounding theoretical statement should be immediately followed by an absurd, slapstick macabre parody of a television panel game (mixing "reality and illusion, sanity and madness, the erotic and the scatological"). What better example of "unconscious mythic residue," the "adolescent thought-mode," and an "exhausted form" than the TV panel game?

But this game, of course, is more than a thin parade of Sunday night celebrities with saccharine smiles and feeble wit; this game deals with "THE BIG QUESTION!" (*P&D*, 80). Ten pages follow in which an unwilling spectator, or Bad Sport, conscripted from the studio audience (the reader observing his own unwilling fate) is badgered by the mock-modest moderator, the Aged Clown, the Lovely Lady, and Mr. America ("fat as the continent and bald as an eagle" [*P&D*, 79], who, having grown fatter and fatter as the game proceeds, finally rips out of his clothes and dies [*P&D*, 85]).

The answer to the big question comes at the end of all the terrifyingly absurd wordplay designed to "lead" Bad Sport to guess the answer to the name of the game. But Bad Sport does not manage to guess the answer—"Much Ado about Nothing." For being unable to guess or to appreciate that life itself is much ado about nothing, that language is a deficient medium with which to consider the enormity of the universe, and that it is the "details" of the game that count, his penalty is "*La Morte!*" (*P&D*, 87). The noose is fitted around the neck of the Bad Sport by the Aged Clown while Lovely Lady coos in his ear and the audience laughs, and then it's "WHAP! . . . So long sport" (*P&D*, 88).

"Panel Game" is the oldest piece in the collection: written in 1957, a dozen years before *P&D*'s publication, it represents "the turning point" for Coover (Andersen, 79). On the surface, the reader may puzzle over this plunge of tone from the highbrow prologue to the TV game, but in fact it contributes to the mix Coover identifies in the prologue as his purpose. His purpose is also to identify new modes of perception and fictional forms to encompass them, to struggle against the unconscious, and to meet the challenge of exhausted form. What better fulfills this than to strike at the heart of the American desire to *be* unconscious, to dissolve in trivia: the TV panel game show? Coover's triumph here is to have transformed this pursuit of mindlessness into a fictional form that itself exposes the game and turns the escape from consciousness into enlightenment.

"The name of the game—is *La Morte*": the death of the mind, of perception. American popular culture creates cliché figures to entertain the public and keep them from understanding their own fate. "I thought it was all for fun," protests the Bad Sport as he is led to his execution (*P&D*, 87) (an execution echoed two collections later in "The Phantom of the Movie Palace" [*ANM*]). His death is reflected in the intellectual death of the society whose entertainment is the pursuit of mental narcosis. Coover's achievement here is the successful reforging of the form of that entertainment itself into a fictional form capable of achieving enlightenment in a dazzlingly dark-comic parody.

"The Marker"
The second oldest piece in the collection, "The Marker" dates from 1959 and is not, in contrast to many of the previous pieces in the book, a

retelling but rather a bizarre, surrealistic metafiction, surely unlike anything that has preceded it in literary history.

A man, Jason, sits with a book in an armchair in his bedroom, while his nude wife prepares for bed. She lies on the bed, "a rhythm of soft white lines on the large white canvas" of the sheet (*P&D*, 89) and smiles at Jason, who places a marker in his book, undresses, shuts off the light, but in the darkness cannot find his way in the room. The furniture seems to have been rearranged. Nor can he get the light to turn on again. He fumbles in the dark, hears his wife's laughter, and finally locates her; his passion is rekindled by the "anxiety" of his disorientation "and its riddles" into "a new urgency, an almost brutal wish to swallow, for a moment, reason and its inadequacies, and to let passion, noble or not, have its hungry way." He enters her, wonders for a moment if this *is* his wife, rejects the absurd fear, leans to kiss her, and notices a "disagreeable odor" (*P&D*, 90).

The lights come on then, and five policemen (mentioned briefly in the first line of the story) barge in. Jason's wife is dead, rotting, has been dead for three weeks, one of the police officers pronounces. Jason, affixed to her, tries desperately to pull free. The policemen force him from her, and one of them beats his genitals to a pulp, whereupon he lectures Jason as to his position on literary theory, a middle position between tradition and innovation, respecting each for its own virtues, but aware of the constant need to review and revise them. Still, the policeman knows that "*some things make me puke!*" (*P&D*, 91) and orders his men to remove the rotting corpse. The officer then notices Jason's book on the table, flips through it, returns it to the table. The marker falls out, and Jason gasps, but the policeman leaves (*P&D*, 92).

The piece is at once amusing and horrifying, and since, despite its chilling moments, it clearly cannot be taken literally, the reader soon realizes its metafictional-allegorical intent. But attempts to interpret its symbolism necessarily become heavy-handed, a bit embarrassing even, ingenious as they may be: "Jason represents every reader whose vision has been limited by an adherence to traditional artistic forms. Like Jason's wife, these forms were once beautiful, but they are now dead and decaying . . . keeping readers like Jason from expanding his literary consciousness. The young man's aesthetic sterility is represented by his penis which he has a difficult time removing from the corpse. . . . Readers who reject alternative possibilities are making love to dead corpses" (Andersen, 25). Lois Gordon attempts to take the piece beyond literary allegory to an allegory of "rigidly routinized lifestyles" (103), but it is difficult to deny the primarily literary content of the police officer's lecture on tradition and innovation even if it is not directly identified as literary. But as Cope points out, this speech is Coover's own parody of his dedicatory prologue to Cervantes (54).

By the absurd exaggeration of the allegorical features, Coover succeeds in concretizing a theoretical dilemma. The exaggeration is hyperbolic comedy, the theorizing dark-comic parody: imagine literary critics in the form of Orwellian policemen barging into people's homes to detach them from their intercourse with dead traditions. Yet, despite the comic macabre extremism, the statement *is* made: as Coover "says" to Cervantes, we need our imagination to be exercised and in good condition (76). Between the direct statement of the prologue and this indirect parody of it, we find the reality Coover is searching for.

Jason's wife is "always at ease" and has a "direct . . . manner of speaking" (*P&D*, 88). In the dark, her image fades for Jason to an undefined abstraction of beauty (*P&D*, 89), and he finds himself lost in the dark, frightened, unable to comprehend what is happening, uncertain for an instant his wife really *is* his wife. Yet the anxiety and riddles produced by this inspire him beyond reason and its inadequacies to passion, "noble or not."

When he discovers that she is in fact a long-dead, rotting corpse, Jason is left impotent, sterile, ultimately bloodied, and alone, having "lost his place." There is no choice left for him but to seek the New World about which Coover speaks to Cervantes in the prologue.

"The Brother"

Coover's inspiration for his biblical retellings solidified when he read a statement by the philosopher Karl Jaspers that led him to perceive the possibility of viewing our biblical heritage not as "literal truth but as story . . . that tells us something, metaphorically, about ourselves and the world" (Andersen, 19). In this light, the biblical retellings show themselves more purely as story than most of the other work in *P&D*. Thus, we come to the third "example" of the fictional styles Coover was working with before moving into his first novel. "The Brother" is neither about fiction nor about the meaning of fictional technique and theory for human identity, but is rather an ironic counterpoint to Genesis 6–9, a story, surely lodged deep in the heart of many a Christian and Jew, about the shadow cast across humanity by God's decisions.

What Bible reader has not wondered about God's dismissal of *all* the citizens of Sodom and Gomorrah aside from His chosen few or, even more extreme, His condemnation of "every imagination of the thoughts of (man's) heart" as "only evil continually" (Genesis 6:5) or the singular favor He shows Noah (Genesis 6:8–9)? Was there truly no one at all among the dismissed, no thought or act by one of them, worthy of praise or admiration?

Enter Noah's brother—as imagined by Coover, a normal man of common decency—with his pregnant wife, equally charitable and unassuming, if a bit disgruntled. Noah's brother narrates the story for us in a good ole boy's twang: he has neglected his own farm to assist his crazed brother in the dubious task of building a boat out in the country, and he has been unable either to dissuade Noah from the project or to abandon him to it. Noah's brother's wife grumbles over this, but acquiesces and provides sandwich lunches not only for her husband but for his brother Noah, whose own wife does not manage to do much for him.

So even though Noah, who is seen by God as perfect and just, has never done much of anything for his brother, the brother helps him at great expense to himself, a good-humored, hard-working, charitable man who realizes finally too late that Noah is *not* mad. The rains come, and at first the brother and his wife are cheered. Their crops and stock will be nourished, they will have a time of much-needed rest together. But the rain continues, the fields are washed out, the flood has begun. The brother goes to Noah to plead for a place for himself and his pregnant wife on the boat they have helped build, but Noah mutely turns his back and enters the boat that only he and his wife and their children and "a whole damn menagerie all clutterin and stinkin up the boat" (*P&D*, 96) may enter. The brother and his wife laughed about the animals at first, but now the brother sees he will be given no mercy by Noah. He swims back to his house and finds his wife drowned. We leave the brother perched on a hill, awaiting his fate, the ark having sailed out of sight.

One of the things Coover does here is shift sympathies from the spiritual to the existential. Clearly God's judgment of humanity was incorrect. At least one good man and his wife are thrown to the flood, their charitable natures manipulated by Noah, their kindness unrewarded. It is difficult to imagine the reader whose sympathy would not shift to Noah's brother in this version of the story. Yet if this is our mythology, then we are descended from Noah the manipulator, not the charitable brother; Noah is the survivor to whom we owe our own survival; he is the one with the ability to curry favor with the authorities, to obtain inside information, to mobilize the work force to action, and to turn his back upon those who have helped him: perhaps a fitting mythology for our world today.

"In a Train Station"

At 9:27, Alfred purchases a ticket for the 10:18 express to Winchester. While he waits, he and the stationmaster exchange banal chat. The narrative voice informs us in advance that Alfred will not be on the train when it leaves ("assuming both Alfred and the Express train to be real" [*P&D*, 99]). Alfred tries at one point to break free of the banal dialogue, which clearly is a kind of script (*P&D*, 101), but is cued in by the stationmaster, who also cues him to take out his lunch. He begins to munch on a chicken leg. A drunk stumbles into the station, drunkenly lectures and prays, blasphemes ("our fasher whish art 'n heaven . . . *is eating hish own goddamn chil'ren!*" [*P&D*, 102]), vomits, faints, rises, falls again. Alfred tries to break his fall but is scolded by the stationmaster.

Weeping, Alfred takes out a knife, puts it to the man's throat, and drops it just as the 10:18 enters the station. The stationmaster takes up the knife and demonstrates to the weeping Alfred how to cut off the drunk's head, disposes of the head and body, and returns to the ticket counter. Alfred, still weeping, has missed his train. The stationmaster sets the clock back to 9:26. Alfred gathers up his things and wearily returns to the ticket window.

In considering this enigmatic example of the state of Coover's art at the time he wrote this story, there is a temptation to make assumptions. Thus, Andersen reminds us that at the end of the piece Alfred, "presumably but not necessarily," will once again buy a ticket for the 10:18 express to Winchester (Andersen, 28). Gordon makes two assumptions, reflected in her comment, "As Alfred again awaits the 10:18 Express, which will never arrive . . . " (106). The "again" is a presumption, not a necessity, and the statement that the train "will never arrive" is an inaccuracy; the train does, in fact (or at any rate, in fiction), arrive and depart, on page 103 ("assuming both Alfred and the Express Train to be real," as Coover mentions early on in the story.

But Alfred, as we are forewarned, is not on the train, although he has bought a ticket for it and will presumably do so again, after the events of the story are completed and the stationmaster sets the clock back to where it was at the beginning of the story, so that they all can presumably experience the same set of events again, as indicated by Alfred's words to the stationmaster when he seeks to depart from an apparently preordained dialogue and begs for a change in script, only to be cued back on course by the stationmaster.

Apparently the stationmaster seeks to teach Alfred to decapitate the drunk, but Alfred cannot and is apparently doomed by his lack of a capacity for brutality to repeat this scene over and over again. The repetition, of course, is only a matter of suggestion, or illusion. In truth, the piece begins and ends and exists only within the confines of its opening and closing sentences as an imagined situation built of words and words only (thus, the query by the narrative voice as to whether or not Alfred and the train are real is, strictly speaking, gratuitous, although interesting).

Is it outworn form that Alfred is forced to repeat again and again until he is able to slay the drunk and ride the train away? In a fiction as brief and evocative and puzzling as this, the reader is tempted to probe every available detail. Why does the drunk speak of God as eating his children? Is this related to Alfred's eating the chicken leg (the ironic fate of life being doomed to consume other life to avoid death)? How does this gastronomical detail relate to the piece and its apparent literary, metafictional intentions? Is the attempt to fathom or explain "God's ways with man" a doomed and drunken effort as old as Milton and as sodden as Houseman ("Malt does more than Milton can / To justify God's ways with man")[9] that we must extinguish before we can move on?

Is it Alfred's pity and sympathy that keep him from his train? Or does the stationmaster hold some other power over him that keeps him locked into the seemingly unending cycle of this exercise? Or is it the author who is the actor here and we, the readers, the victims, doomed to read and reread an endless series of repetitions of banal scenes into which we are locked by the inability of our own hearts to strike beyond pity and put an end to the preconceptions governing our art?

"Klee Dead"

On first reading, this cryptic little piece may seem more like an exercise than a "story." The narrator begins by telling us about the death of a man named Klee (or who *might* be named Klee) by a fall, quite likely a suicide. The narrator soon digresses to tell us about Millicent Gee, who lives alone in a basement with a ram, cats, and some dead fish. After a page of Millie, the narrator confesses that she has nothing to do with Klee and he does not know why he mentioned her in the first place. He returns to the narration of Klee.

"Who was Klee? I do not know. I do not care." The reader is invited to assume he died as a result of the fall, though he may have died "to save physics" (*P&D*, 107). Again he digresses to talk about another man, named Orval Nulin Evachefsky, who jumps to his death at the age of 42 because he mistakenly believes that he has infected his pregnant wife with syphilis from an earlier sexual encounter. He is impaled on a parking meter into which yet another character, named Carlyle Smith, is about to insert a penny. That is all we are told about Carlyle Smith.

The narration then moves to the firemen scraping up the remains of Klee from the sidewalk. One of the firemen gathers up broken bits of denture in a little pouch and inadvertently farts. We then learn that Orval suffered from a mental disturbance marked by melancholy. Whether Klee's suicide was the result of a mere disease of his private reason or "reason itself was Klee's disease, we will never know" (*P&D*, 111). The story then ends with an apology.

The narrator himself expected more, he explains, and offers the reader some circus tickets (which, it has earlier been suggested, the narrator tried in vain to use as a bribe to the city clerk to get more information about Klee, although it is difficult to know whether this is merely another throwaway joke).

There is a fascination to the piece. Coover skillfully holds the reader's attention despite the seemingly rambling nature of his nonstory and the chill indifference of the narrator to the details of the two deaths he tells us about.

What is Coover up to here? Is he simply systematically fracturing fictional tradition, eliminating coherence, linearity, plot, cause and effect (other than death being caused by a fall from a high place, confirming physics), and all but the most rudimentary details of characterization in order to demonstrate that story exists as a result of the mere facts of life and its cessation? For the very absence of coherence, the very randomness and arbitrary nature of the events related seem finally to infuse the story with a realism beyond literary technique. "Klee Dead" imitates reality far more closely than fictional realism purports to; Coover gives us life as physics. When we fall, we die. Life is little more than a mass of random details, some of which are the cause of further detail, others of which lead nowhere. Aside from that, there are a couple of tickets to the circus. "What is life, after all," the narrator asks, "but a caravan of lifelike forgeries?" (*P&D*, 111)

Coover's only obligation is to interest us in reading this and wondering what it means. He has fulfilled his part. The rest is up to us.

"J's Marriage"

With the sixth of the seven exemplary fictions we return to the Bible, this time to a retelling of the Immaculate Conception story. The difference here is that, as in "The Brother," we get the story not through the point of view of the principals (Mary and Jesus, who remain unnamed and, in Jesus' case, unseen) but through that of J, the shadowy figure who in biblical accounts and manger plays is generally depicted as standing around holding Mary's dog, as it were. Calling the Joseph figure J evokes a Kafkaesque picture of this intelligent, introspective man in the shadow of the highest authority.

The older, more intelligent, educated, and experienced J professes love and adoration to a younger woman who returns his professions "in kind, though rarely with such intensity." He adores her but questions the nature of his adoration—was it merely "the objectification of a possible adorable?" The worldly, somewhat cynical J fears "the ultimate misery of any existence, the inevitable disintegration of love, the hastening process of physical and mental rot, the stupidity of human passion" (*P&D*, 112).

Nonetheless, he proposes marriage. She is shocked; he has wooed her with words and suspects that she fears he is nothing more than words. Atypically, he grows angry and presses her, and she tears away, spitting out at him hatefully, whereupon he sinks into melancholy, "unable to lift a hammer or turn a blade" (he *is*, you see, a carpenter). She seeks him out again; he renews his proposal; again, she turns from him. So it continues until he begins to understand that she fears the love act itself. He speculates as to what might have caused this ("misguided dehortations . . . some early misadventure . . . a dominant father" [*P&D*, 113]); obsessed with her, he proposes that they marry without sex until such time as she might encourage his attentions. She grasps that with this man she will always have the upper hand in matters of sex and "All right, she said. All right, yes" (*P&D*, 114) (in a thin, ironic echo of Molly Bloom's famous, joyous surrender).[10]

They marry, and despite his doubts, fears, submerged impatience, and general view of the universe (*P&D*, 114), J enjoys several months of incredible happiness. They encounter "an emotional harmony, inexpressibly beautiful" (*P&D*, 115), and the chaste nature of their marriage seems finally a minor detail that will ultimately be resolved. He perceives the potential of beauty in the world through his perception of her. Their intimacy increases slowly, but he is tortured by his unfulfilled desire for her and envies the water she bathes in, the chair he carves for her to sit on (perhaps another echo of Joyce, this time of Leopold Bloom: "happy the chair beneath her").[11]

Then one evening she appears naked before him at bedtime, but only to tell him she is pregnant (*P&D*, 116). Stunned, J falls ill. She nurses him. She explains to him that her pregnancy is an act of God, which explanation he accepts, although he "couldn't imagine whatever had brought a God to do such a useless and . . . almost vulgar thing" (*P&D*, 117). He ponders it

41

feverishly, trying to understand how God would involve himself in the affairs of a human animal; but he cannot understand and finally gives it up. Then his health begins to improve.

As his situation improves, hers worsens, and he cares for her, growing in stature with his selflessness. She, for her part, shows great courage, suffers with dignity "the great misfortune of the ill-timed trip [Coover need elaborate no details here, we all know them] . . . the flesh-ripping agony of birth, writhing on the dirt floor like a dying beast, yet noble, beautiful" (*P&D*, 117–18).

At this point, I think, we find the key to the story and to the character of J, and in this, I believe this story is set apart in its spiritual intent from "The Brother."

"It was—that moment of the strange birth—J's most mystic moment, his only undisputable glimpse of the whole of existence, yet one which he later renounced, needless to say, later understood in the light of his overwrought and tortured emotions. And it was also the climax of his love for her; afterwards, they drifted quietly and impassively apart, until in later years J found himself incapable even of describing her to himself or to another person" (*P&D*, 118).

J is indifferent to the child and the child to J. "J grew to prefer not being bothered to any other form of existence" (*P&D*, 118). Finally, then, after he has lost his great passion for his wife, one evening (or perhaps it is only a dream), he does make love to her, though the "penetration" is little more than an addition to his customary routine of bathing her. Clearly the moment is an anticlimactic one.

J dies, an old man, "with his face in a glassful of red wine," and his thoughts are "that life had turned out to be nothing more or less than he had expected after all. . . . [M]ost important of all . . . in spite of everything, there was nothing tragic about it, no, nothing to get wrought up about, on the contrary" (*P&D*, 119). Then, in a moment of extraordinary literary beauty, an image comes to his mind, a memory of how his wife fell asleep the morning following their wedding night. He laughs the shrill note of an old man, then dies.

This tale can be differentiated from the other exemplary biblical retelling, "The Brother," in that, although it too recounts the consequences of an act of God in the life of a "minor" character, the characterization here is more complex and considerably more literary, even Jamesian.

In Andersen's interpretation, "Joseph has been hurt and abused by the vulgar act for which God is responsible" (22). But I think that is only half, the more superficial half, of this complex and beautiful story. Noah's brother's fate is an ironic one; he dies, despite his goodness, as a consequence of an apparently incorrect judgment by God. But J's fate results from his own nature, from the choices he makes to reject beauty. Repeatedly throughout the story, J rejects the moments of spiritual illumination he encounters and infuses every perception of beauty with doubt. Despite his disclaimer at the end that it is *not* so, there is in fact a real element of tragedy in his fate, engendered by his pride in his own consciousness, which leads him to refuse to allow himself any surrender to the spirit or to passions greater than his desire for his virginal wife.

J is essentially a man of words and doubt. He doubts that she understands "the most beautiful things he said to her" beyond the emotion behind them (*P&D*, 112). In the first months of their virginal marriage, J is happier than he has ever been, and this happiness reaches the point of revelation of the beauty of the world. But even as this beauty is revealed to him, instantly his intellect intervenes: "It was *not* beautiful, no, it would be absurd to think of this or any other natural composite as beautiful, but it was as though it *could* be beautiful, as though somewhere there resided within it the potentiality of beauty . . . only illusion of course" (*P&D*, 115).

And again, the night of the birth (and has the Nativity ever been depicted more starkly and more beautifully?), when his wife writhes on the dirt floor "like a dying beast, yet noble, beautiful," is "J's most mystic moment, his only indisputable glimpse of the whole of existence." Yet he *does* dispute it, renounces it even. To see beauty is to be "overwrought" emotionally. And from this final rejection, his life goes downhill the rest of the way. He comes to prefer a life of indifference, prefers above all not to be bothered. Nothing remains for him but dullness and indifference—indifference to his son, even to the consummation of his marriage.

J professes to be surprised that God can be other than indifferent to the affairs of men and finds it vulgar that God has impregnated his wife. Thus, his arrogance is of heroic proportions: he does not disbelieve in God, but his faith in his own intellect is greater than his faith in the judgement of God. In some way, by virtue of his indifference, he seems to view himself as *superior* to God. Yet for all his faith in the powers of his own intellect, he never manages to become aware of his own consistent unwillingness to receive the enlightenment that comes his way or to admit to the existence of a beauty in existence greater than the scope of his intellect, even when it is made evident to his heart.

Thus, J's tragedy finally is not one inflicted upon him by God's indifference, but by his own indifference to or perhaps fear of beauty. J is a man too steeped in his own words and intellect to release himself to illuminations greater than those achieved by his own mind. In the end, he is resigned to it all and dies, ironically, in a glass of red wine, an echo of the blood of the son whose coming to give his life for mankind (the ultimate opposite of indifference) only leaves his surrogate father cold.

J is a modernist figure, a Prufrock, a Dubliner, James's John Marcher in "The Beast in the Jungle" (1901). Coover's innovation here is to have shaped, from the sparse materials of the Gospel story in question, this very human story of intellectual tragedy.

"The Wayfarer"

The narrator, wearing a badge and carrying a rifle, stops on the road before an apparently impoverished, possibly stunned, silent old man in worn, dirty clothes, seated on "an old milestone" by the wayside (*P&D*, 120). The wayfarer's eyes are covered with the dust of the road, but the narrator succeeds in getting them to register his presence, nothing more. He wonders if the man has seen his badge, if he is fearful, indifferent, or even contemptuous. Agitated, the narrator takes out his notebook, finds it blank, urgently writes in it, is relieved, and concludes the man is afraid.

The narrator tries in many ways to provoke a response from the wayfarer: he pokes him with his rifle, shouts, orders him to sit, to stand, stamps on his feet, breaks his nose with the rifle butt, squats down and orders the man to stay exactly as he is, orders the man's nose to keep bleeding—but he finds no satisfaction in the compliance with these last orders.

The narrator has orders that apparently allow him to execute the wayfarer at his discretion (he has "unlimited authority"). He contemplates where to shoot the wayfarer, head or chest; finally deciding on the chest, he shoots him there. The wayfarer begins to bleed and finally to speak "rapidly, desperately with neither punctuation nor sentence structure . . . a ceaseless eruption of obtuse language" (*P&D*, 123). The narrator becomes annoyed and shoots him again, in the head, finishing him off. The narrator returns to his patrol car and calls in the details of the incident, writes it up in his memo book, turns from the messy corpse, and imagines the man as he was when he first saw him—as a prelude to forgetting him. Yet the narrator sits there in his car a little longer, his mind "not yet entirely free of the old man." "At times he would loom in my inner eye larger than the very landscape . . . my motives had been commendable, of course, but the consequences of such a gesture, if practiced habitually, could well prove disastrous. I would avoid it in the future" (*P&D*, 124).

He watches the traffic and becomes absorbed in the flow and "its unbroken grace and precision. There was a variety in detail but the stream itself was one" (*P&D*, 124). With this thought his mind is freed, and he enters the flow himself, calm and happy, a participant, a man who enjoys his work.

This brief tale, the last of the "Seven Exemplary Fictions," is as evocative and cryptic as any of them. Gordon says, "The story is about the inadequacy of capturing the richness of experience with language," although she erroneously reports that stripping off the wayfarer's many thick coats (which she interprets as symbols of "the structures imposed on him") is the trigger that releases his random speech (110). In fact, the narrator resists the urge to remove the coats, and the old man's speech finally breaks free only when the coats are soaked through with the blood from his bullet wounds.

Andersen interprets the story in light of an intriguing statement by William H. Gass that the principal function of popular culture is to keep men from understanding what is happening to them: Andersen sees the wayfarer as a character who has withdrawn from one social activity after another (presumably an interpretation of the metaphor of his "many coats") and who thus is "less and less alienated from his authentic self," though also seemingly "almost comatose" (26, 27). Interesting though this interpretation may be, it does seem to be built more on speculation than on concrete reference to the text.

Who or what *is* the wayfarer? A man who travels on foot, stops at the side of the road, sits on a milestone—an *old* milestone—and is under investigation by the authorities. No attempt to make him speak or explain himself is successful, and his utter nonresponsiveness plays heavily on the nerves of his interrogator, enough to evoke execution on the spot. The narrator is troubled by his own action, even though he has been authorized to carry it out, albeit not necessarily on the spot. It takes him some moments before he can free himself of the messy image of the man he has killed, but he seems more troubled by the messiness of it than by the fact that he has killed someone. He does not like shooting people in the head because he does "not enjoy the sight of mutilated heads" (*P&D*, 123), even though he sees it as a more humane method of execution. Further, he finds his own motives "commendable"—to perform his duty, his function.

What seems to trouble the narrator most about the wayfarer is that he is not a part of the mainstream and will not explain himself. He represents the empty memo pad, the blank page, lack of understanding, a threat to the unity and uniformity of the mainstream represented by the traffic flowing past. One either participates in that movement or must be eliminated. The function of the narrator is to do the eliminating, "regardless how disagreeable it may be." Passersby appreciate his situation; he returns their smiles of "commiseration" "with a pleasant nod" (*P&D*, 120).

The narrator steps out of the flow, performs his duty by killing the old man, and returns to the flow. The stream cannot tolerate the individual, cannot accept that which will neither explain itself nor respond to the prodding query, that which merely is.

The piece is many-faceted and open to many interpretations—that it is about the inadequacy of language; about the danger of being a witness, of not participating; about the consequences of participating in the mindless flow; about the silence of the authentic self and its unnerving effect on the vulnerable conformist; even about the loss of humanity of the automobile society and the triumph of the machine over man. One might even view the old man as the many-coated mute of outworn literary traditions, slain by a writer doing his job.

But finally, I think, the story has a certain sphinxlike quality. Like the old man himself garbed in his many cloaks and seated on an old milestone, "The Wayfarer" will not explain itself, no matter how we poke and prod and jostle it. The explanations must be our own. If the blank pages of our memo book unnerve us, we must fill them ourselves.

"The Elevator"

In 15 numbered scenes, we follow Martin's various experiences as, "without so much as reflecting upon it" (*P&D*, 125), he takes the elevator every morning to the fourteenth floor where he works. Sometimes the elevator is self-service; sometimes it has an elevator girl.

In scene 1, having arrived early, Martin impulsively pushes the button for the basement, where he has never before ventured. He is overtaken by a sense of "gloom and loss" and imagines he is descending into hell, but the door yawns open, and there is nothing there, only a basement, "silent and meaningless." He presses 13: "Hell's the other way!" (*P&D*, 126). In scene 2 he is humiliated on the elevator by a man named Carruther, who farts silently and blames it on Martin, to the amusement of the others in the car: "Who fahred that shot? . . . Mart fahred it!' . . . Is that Martin fartin again?" Martin is helpless to defend himself and can only glance apologetically at the elevator girl. Seething with hatred, he secretly plans revenge.

In scene 3 Martin is alone in the elevator with the girl, a scene that stutters like a fantasy trying to establish its most appealing scenario. As the girl grasps the lever, the elevator "cage sighs upward" and Martin shifts from stance to stance, friendly to shy to gallant to cool to hot. The very brief scene 4 speculates about the possibility of Martin meeting death in the dark silent shaft one day: "He will not protest.... He will protest.... He will not protest" (*P&D*, 128) (an echoing of Beckett's "I can't go on. I must go on. I go on"?)

In scene 5, Martin serves as a silent philosophical guardian to the other passengers as the elevator ascends and they depart to their various floors, until he is finally alone; then he too departs, and the car is empty. In scene 6 Martin and the girl are alone in the elevator when the cable snaps and the car plunges. He lies on the floor and gets her to lie on top of him to cushion her body from the crash; strokes her as the elevator whistles, dropping.

In scene 7, Martin is working late in his office and discovers that his watch has stopped—it is past midnight. He leaves and goes to the elevator, which rises toward him with a grieving plaint (*P&D*, 131). He presses the button for 1, but the car rises to 15—"There *is* no fifteenth floor!" Martin steps out into the cold darkness there, and the elevator descends with an "amused rumble" (*P&D*, 132) as he attempts, in vain, to recall it, feeling some other presence there in the dark with him. In scene 8, again bullied and teased by Carruther, he strikes back: "Carruther fucks his mother," he says, and Carruther punches him, breaking his glasses (*P&D*, 132). Martin feels the girl shrink from him as the others laugh.

Scene 9 is a very brief return to the fantasy of the falling elevator, with the girl, who has now removed her skirt, in the embrace of Martin, who wonders how it will feel (the crash? or the sex? or both?). Scene 10 depicts typical morning stress among people going to work: "deformed brow-beaten mind animals. Their foolish anxiety seeps out like a bad spirit.... Tyrannized by their own arbitrary regimentation of time. Torture self-imposed, yet in all probability inescapable" (*P&D*, 134, 137).

Scene 11 is a three-line proclamation of Martin's omnipotence as he damns the elevator, a destructive force. In scene 12 the elevator "shrieks insanely as it drops," and again Martin and the girl, naked now, embrace. "He thrusts up off the plummeting floor." Scene 13 is an unattributed statement (by Martin presumably, though possibly by the author) of detached superior regard of the doomed: "[L]et their flesh sag and dewlaps tremble . . . let them laugh . . . let them cry!" (*P&D*, 134).

In scene 14 a colloquial narrator describes a transformed Martin ("Mort" or "Mert"), who has a five-foot "doodang" that pops up under his chin "like the friggin eye of god" (*P&D*, 136), knocking Carruther out and causing the elevator girl to faint. Scene 15 opens with a fragment of the falling embrace. It also includes another cryptic fragment of proclamation by Martin of the indestructible seed and a final paragraph in which Martin, "reflecting upon it for once" (*P&D*, 137) (in contrast to the opening and repeated refrain, "without so much as reflecting upon it" (*P&D*, 125, 129, 133), takes the stairs instead of the elevator, "out of a strange premonition." Halfway up, he hears the elevator hurtle by him and crash below. "Inscrutable," he decides and continues to climb the stairs, staring back down behind him from time to time.

This fiction is dazzlingly written, crafted, and paced. It is comic and frightening, lucid and perplexing, in many ways simple, yet overwhelmingly complex. The reader moves through it with eager anticipation and continuing surprise and finishes the piece in uncertainty, with many questions.

How many lives do we have? How many strands of life, or faces? How many segments of our life constitute a series of events that are a life unto themselves? How much of our life is sheer quotidian repetition, varied only by the flickers of our private thoughts and fantasies? How many ways do we have of telling the story of our life? Every day we rise, eat, go to work, return home, eat, sleep, rise, and so on. Every day we get into the car or onto the bus, enter a building, an elevator, enter a world of strangers. Life is a series of repetitions and internal reflections. How many ways are there to tell a story, *this* story, *our* story?

Each of the 15 fragments that constitute "The Elevator" shows a variation within a frame of repetition. Within the narrow confines of his life and his personality, we see Martin each day, unreflecting, ride the elevator to his office—a poor excuse for a quest (an echo perhaps of Coover's address to Cervantes, "the nag's a pile of bones"? [*P&D*, 78]), which nonetheless sends him through a range of fictional fragments, confrontations, nightmares, and erotic adventures. He is helpless, yearning, tyrannized by his life, locked into time. Suicide sings its siren song to him in the abyss of the shaft. The elevator girl fondling the lever that makes the car rise excites his fantasy and desire; he dreams of holding her, of making love to her as the car plunges to a crash. Or is it a dream? Isn't it all a dream? A fiction? It is impossible to determine here with certainty whether the realistic frame is meant to be real or a frame. The "progress" in the "story" seems an ironic concession: Martin begins, unreflecting, riding the elevator every day, ends for once reflecting, and forgoes the elevator only to hear it crash down the shaft as he climbs the stairs.

What is the elevator? It is a cell of human consciousness, a womb, a vehicle of all experience, a conveyance down to the silent hell of the basement and up to the hell of the quotidian, or further up to the dimension of timeless nonexistence. It is a machine, it is a consciousness, it is acted upon, it itself acts.

Who is Martin? To Gordon, he is committed and optimistic (102), to Andersen, he is "a dullard" (99), "forever conventional and impotent" (101). He is both these types and more—a philosopher, a pathetic daydreamer, a discontent, a hesitant adventurer yearning to explore the basement, a meek victim with the heart of an avenging god. Unreflecting, he rides the elevator daily; when finally he reflects, he takes the stairs and hears the elevator crash, saved by a premonition. Martin is a knot of many strands of character and as such is perhaps closer to the reality of human character, far rounder and more comprehensive of human identity than the traditional "round" character of literature as identified by Forster (Forster, chapter 4).

Martin's story, the story of the elevator, is a conglomerate of the comprehensive range of ideas, emotions, and possibilities embodied in everyone, the flow of contradictions that in traditional fiction is unacceptably confusing and anti-illusionary but here serves to make the fiction ever more complete and complex. His is also the story of our poor daily venture into the world, the hoard of risks that surround us, the ever-changing flaming sun of our mind-soul burning through one idea, one pose, one mask, one wish, one thought after another, sending up mythic images in the guise of daydream and in comic dialect, the daily choice that is our escape from death.

Martin is, in comic narration, a god of creation (scene 14), a god of destruction (scenes 11 and 13), the death-defying hero of a recurring romantic adventure (scenes 3, 9, 12, 14, and 15), a daydreamer, an existential hero, and a working stiff. Scene 7 suggests a dimension of timelessness, a place that does not exist as long as clocks measure our days and work for us; it is a frightening place, a place to which he is delivered and where he is left by an elevator car whose machines sound a "grinding plaint" as it comes for him and leaves him with "an amused rumble."

In scene 3 his identity shifts rapidly (he is friendly, gallant, cool, passionate) as the scene stutters forward to give him the mask he needs to win (or achieve the necessary verisimilitude of the fantasy to allow him to dream that he wins) the girl, whose fondling of the lever sparks his desire. He is a naive con man using disaster as a ruse to get the elevator girl down on her back. Or he is a fertility god (scene 12) inspiring awe with an enormous phallus, the envy of men and terror of women.

In the final two glimpses of his copulation in the falling car, he "thrusts up off the plummeting floor" and again (scene 15) proclaims the indestructible seed, the thrust and proclamation of the urge to continue the race even in the face of imminent death. But then, suddenly, there is a shift, he reflects "for once," and in reflecting escapes death.

This escape might well be from the death of being locked into the mindless daily routine, but it also echoes our literal daily escape from the possibility of our death. Every day we make a series of choices, split-second pauses, hesitations, and turns that guide us forward in life away from the fall, the knife, the rope that snaps, the object that drops, the speeding automobile that might bring death; we escape, looking back over our shoulder from time to time at the fate that we have left behind, but that also lies "inscrutably" before us. Martin's escape is effected by reflection. He thinks, chooses consciously, and finds an alternative that delivers him from the fate of the other "mind animals."

The details of this piece are so tightly interwoven, the writing so exquisitely precise, that, like the supreme artistry of a dream, it is an insuperable task to attempt to catalog all of its amazements. Its power simply continues: "It goes on, ever giving birth to itself. Up and down. Up and down" (*P&D*, 133, 34).

"The Romance of the Thin Man and the Fat Lady"
This fiction begins with an observation about the obvious symbolism of the humorous coupling of a tall bony man and a fleshy woman, a natural romantic pair ("We are all Thin Men. You are all Fat Ladies" [*P&D*, 138]). But the Thin Man and the Fat Lady are unhappy. The pair has become a triangle with the intrusion of the Ringmaster, "keeper of the Holier Books," who will allow neither the Fat Lady to lose weight to please the Thin Man nor the Thin Man to develop muscle to please the Fat Lady. Doing so would also improve their health, but if "the Fat Lady were not the fattest and the Thin Man the thinnest in the world ... no one would pay to see them ... the circus collapses, and we're all out on the street" (*P&D*, 140–41).

But unhappiness causes the Fat Lady to lose her appetite, and she begins to waste away; the Thin Man stops eating altogether. Before she becomes completely worthless, the devious and sinister Ringmaster trades her for "an Ambassador from Mars and a small sum of money." Outraged, the circus rises up against the Ringmaster, executes and buries him ("castrating him symbolically in the process—circus people are born to symbology" [*P&D*, 141]), and reinstalls the Fat Lady and the Thin Man.

Happiness reigns again, the circus prospers, and they learn that the show can function without a Ringmaster: "acts coming on spontaneously ... wild and exciting and unpredictable ... open-ended" (*P&D*, 142). But as the Fat Lady and the Thin Man slim down and muscle up, respectively, in the interests of love, health, and happiness, the spectators begin to lose interest. Finally, no one in the circus can "ignore the black and white truth of the circus ledger. . . . Somewhere, apparently, there is a fatter lady and a thinner man" (*P&D*, 143).

Under group pressure, the Fat Lady and Thin Man begin to try to fatten back up and slim back down, respectively, for the good of the circus, but it is a bitterly ironic situation: "Disgusted by her fat, she is disgusted she has added so little of it. . . . Disgusted by his thinness, he is disgusted that he still wears those little pouches (of muscle) under his skin" (*P&D*, 143–44). They monitor one another's progress and begin to bicker, even to hate each other; "their gloom spreads like wet sawdust through the whole circus. Gate receipts diminish" (*P&D*, 145).

The Thin Man "renegotiates the old deal with the rival circus, and before anyone realizes what has happened, they have an Ambassador from Mars in their midst, and the Fat Lady is gone" (*P&D*, 145). The Thin Man takes power and grows ruthless, the circus now is "without pleasure ... dismal, shadowy ... who can wander through ... without a taste of dread?" The others turn against the Thin Man; he "is exiled to the rival circus in exchange for a Family of Webfooted Midgets" (*P&D*, 146)—all this happens in the interests of rescuing the narrator's "unhinged" metaphor (and the circus's economic viability). The Thin Man, of course, is being sent back to his love. They rush into one another's arms to the rejoicing of all spectators and circus people.

"Yet somehow ... [the metaphor] has lost its charm ... having gone to such limits to reunite them, we are irritated to discover their limits, to find that the Ludicrous is not also Beautiful." It seems there should be more or "perhaps it is ourselves who are corrupted ... [who have] watched too many parades ... safely witnessed too many thrills ... lost a taste for the simple" (*P&D*, 147).

The narrator reminds us that the Fat Lady and the Thin Man are not *all* the circus has to offer and draws our attention to the other attractions—"half-human half-reptile ... lives entirely on human flesh ... cottoncandy popcawn sodypop ... thrillsnchills" (*P&D*, 148), and on up to "the first ring feachuh act, the tumblin twosome from Tuskyloosa" riding on a rocket high above without a net. "Those flirters with death" turn out to be none other than the Thin Man and the Fat Lady riding on a rocket: "Haw haw givum a big hand folks ... *look out!*" (*P&D*, 149).

The conflict begins here when these two conventional figures, the Thin Man and the Fat Lady (the only possible metaphor, the narrator points out—it cannot be thin lady and fat man or any other combination), decide to change their identities. The Ringmaster, "keeper of the Holier Books" (namely, the accounts, which are "holier" than all books, presumably including literary ones), must whip them back into shape—or rather into their traditional *mis*-shape, which draws the crowds and sells the tickets, beauty, health, happiness, and love be damned.

Even the revolution and assassination of the Ringmaster cannot for long change these facts. The vulgar crowd casts the deciding vote in the form of ticket purchases. In the face of economic collapse, love turns to hatred, disgust, and self-disgust between the Fat Lady and the Thin Man. Ultimately, even the Thin Man himself comes to understand these economic facts, and this understanding enables him to seize power, which power he employs to sell off the Fat Lady. He grows a moustache and procures a whip, but like the Ringmaster before him, he drives too hard, is too ruthless. The circus loses pleasure, and the Thin Man is overpowered, sold off, too, but back into the arms of his long-lost Fat Lady.

Love triumphs, for a time; reunited, they inspire joy, but again not for long. Their charm wanes. After all this, they are too clearly ludicrous, and they are not beautiful. More is needed, and at last they must beef up their act after all by making it more complex and dangerous: defying death, they ride a rocket high up in the big top, no net beneath them.

Vulgarity triumphs. Economic survival is the art of arts and will always be contingent upon vulgar expectation and demand. Health, happiness, love, beauty, and freedom will always take the backseat. A tad obvious, and touted as such, the metafiction here is thin by comparison with other stronger pieces in the volume. Restricted perhaps by the single metaphor, "The Romance of the Thin Man and the Fat Lady" lacks the greater power of mystery inherent in the uncertainty and complexities of pieces like "The Magic Poker," "The Elevator," and the next few we will consider—perhaps because the blend of metafiction, realism, and the absurd is multidimensional in these other pieces, while this thin romance is as limited in scope as the circus itself. Or perhaps we have lost our taste for the simple? Have we seen too many parades of technique?

"Quenby and Ola, Swede and Carl"

This remarkable fiction consists of 38 compact scenes with no transitional connectives, presented from varying points of view and involving four characters: Quenby and Swede, a married couple who run a small lodge; Ola, their teenage daughter; and Carl, a guest at the resort who is an office worker in from the city for a week or two of fishing.

In a boat stalled on the lake at night sit Carl and Swede. On the shore Quenby and Ola are at the barbecue pit preparing dinner—or is Swede with them? Is the latter scene simultaneous with the former? Or is it another's imagining? There is a flashback of a sexual encounter on an old bed in one of the cabins. Carl knows many of the natural details of the lake islands, the birds and flora, but does not quite know where he is now in the darkness. He tries to chat with Swede in the boat but evokes little response. On shore Ola is telling a story about her cat and her father, delightfully imitating his laconic ways; "she enjoyed being at the center of attention and told the story well" (*P&D*, 152).

As the scenes unfold from the different points of view, the story that emerges is one in which Carl apparently has had sex with Quenby (or is it a fantasy?), has gone skinny-dipping, and possibly more, with Ola (or is it a fantasy?), and is now in a stalled boat out on the lake with their husband and father, Swede. Swede is the kind of man, we learn via Ola's story, who, pokerfaced, could throw his daughter's cat up in the air and shoot its head off for tracking through a pie in the kitchen, a man who has perhaps been *too* close to nature, too isolated for too long. There is a strain of uncertainty as to whether the boat has really stalled or Swede knows about Carl and his wife and is planning to do something in the dark on the lake.

In the "deep stillness [that] prevails, a stillness and darkness unknown to the city" (*P&D*, 153), the boat drifts on the lake while Swede tinkers with the motor and Carl's imagination putters with scenarios (or perhaps he is merely remembering). All the while he feels vaguely out of place, questions why he has come, is uncertain if he even really likes being there, misses his warm home, TV, drinks, and hot suppers, and worries about his ignorance of country ways, his incompetence and helplessness exposed before Swede.

The scene fragments come in spurts to create this uncertain picture, including Ola's story of her father's brutal killing of her cat. At the close of the fiction, we get the final detail of that story: the sound the cat made hitting the ground after Swede threw it in the air and shot it, a fluttering sound Ola cannot forget. Though she tells the story without rancor, with good humor, even laughing about Swede's sarcasm (he gave the cat a chance, he says, by throwing it in the air—if it had flown away he wouldn't have shot it), still she remembers that sound as she lies in bed amid the noises of the country at night, listening to "men in boats out on the lake, arguing, chattering, opening beercans. Telling stories" (*P&D*, 167).

Since the fiction ends with no clarification no resolution, the reader is forced to investigate why the piece is so compelling and haunting and what its focus is. Like numerous other pieces in the volume, the story is a metafiction: it focuses on the process of storytelling and on the faculty of imagination. Many of the scene fragments stem from the imaginations of the characters themselves. Ola tells her story, imitates her father, enjoys her art. Carl, in the boat in the dark, imagines (or recreates in memory?) himself with Quenby, with Ola; imagines a body hooked on the boat's line, dragged, dead, underwater like a great fish; imagines Swede intends to kill him, perhaps even merely *imagines* Swede himself (just as the author does). "A man can imagine a lot of things, alone on a strange lake in a dark night" (*P&D*, 163).

So we have an imagined fiction peopled by characters whose imaginings provide the scene fragments that constitute the fiction. And finally we have Ola in bed in the dark wondering about the meaning of the story she has told about her father and the cat, the story she tells as an entertainment but the final mortal detail of which she has withheld. And breathing the "profound silence" of the night within which she ponders the memory that haunts her are the sounds of animals and of men, "telling stories" (*P&D*, 167).

Against these metafictional elements, we have the details borrowed from conventional, melodramatic forms: a triangle, the menacing hunting guide, the menacing husband, the sex-starved country wife, the awkward city man, a stalled boat on a dark lake, the general air of menace expertly suggested by the merest touches of detail. Were these evocative and cozily mysterious elements handled differently, more conventionally, they might add up to a good yarn, a murder mystery, a plotted, even moralistic, thriller, perhaps with a lucid meaning: the corrupted man of the city, having taken advantage of the country wife, is punished by the country man.

But the reader has no way of knowing what the story per se *means*, or even what it *is*, much less what it means. Rather, attention is focused on the myriad fictional possibilities inherent in the series of scenes—a scattering of brilliant fragments that give tantalizing glimpses of a whole that cannot quite be fitted together, yet that somehow leave us with a fiction more stirring than a conventional one, a fiction that evokes the terror and complexity and tantalizing shadows of life itself. With no plot, coherent transition, explanation, or resolution, the essence of this mystery is its insolubility.

"The Sentient Lens"

"Scene for 'Winter'"

The first of the second set of fictions that illustrate the existential and fictional ideas with which Coover was working between 1957 and 1962, "Scene for 'Winter'" begins with "no sound," or rather, "an inappreciable crackle [that] our ear . . . hears [as] the absence of sound . . . reaches out past any staticky imperfections . . . and finds: only the silence" (*P&D*, 168). Snow is falling. Does it fold itself into drifts or is the earth itself ribbed beneath? "We cannot know, we can be sure only of the surface we see now" (*P&D*, 168–69). The eye of the lens follows the snow and the light until suddenly a sound seizes the attention, then another: the sound "of snow being crushed underfoot" (*P&D*, 169). A rabbit appears and disappears, followed by a dog hunting it. Our eye continues to search, discovers we are not in the woods but in a park, and finds a road. A horse-drawn sleigh bursts upon the scene and races by "in a turbulence of blinding snow" (*P&D*, 170), leaving behind a man who is smiling. The eye observes him in intricate detail as he approaches us. The background fades slowly to white.

There is only the man "striding furiously across a barren expanse of shadowless shapes" (*P&D*, 171). He stops, smokes a cigarette, checks to be sure he is alone and urinates. "He writes in the snow as he relieves himself—but we cannot discover the words—or rather we can make them out plainly, but afterwards we cannot remember them..." The man is laughing, but we cannot hear it, "silence still governs our consciousness." He "collapses to his knees and scribbles in the snow with his finger: 'I DID THIS!'" (*P&D*, 173). He falls down laughing, and we hear it now; but we also notice the man's face is somber as he laughs. He is, in fact, terrified, and we see then that the smile is painted on and he is actually weeping. The man's lips seem to be reciting a word over and over, but we cannot hear it; we hear only the sudden sound of his retching.

We swoop back from the man, leaving him "coiled in the snow, helpless like a beetle" (*P&D*, 173), to the comforting shadows of the forest; suddenly we think we see him again, but it is the white rabbit, "its mouth split in a sardonic grin . . . between the jaws of the . . . dog." We hear the crackle of bones as the dog munches them, but that sound too diminishes, disappears, "absorbed into the transcendent silence of winter. Snow again begins to fall" (*P&D*, 174).

Thus ends the scene, leaving the reader to ponder, or cooperate in the creation of, its meaning. Something about the scene is reminiscent of the demonstration records phonograph manufacturers used to produce to illustrate the qualities of a stereophonic set: sound switched from the left speaker to the right, the sound of marching soldiers or of sleigh bells seeming to pass by us from left to right. So, too, this scene produces auditory illusions, though it uses no high-tech tools. Here our ears learn to transcend "any staticky imperfections . . . and (hear) only the silence."

Other sounds seize our attention—the sound of wood freezing, snow being crushed underfoot, sleigh bells. But throughout "silence still governs our consciousness," and what we never hear in the piece is "human" speech. The single human character who appears mouths words we never hear; all we hear of him is the sound of his retching.

Two of our senses are evoked in this scene. It is as though we are watching a silent film, or a film whose sound system is primitive, faulty. We hear silence by convention, as it were, and ignore the static beneath, and we see only surfaces—is the snow ribbed or the ground it covers? What we never hear or see are human words (aside, of course, from the words of the story itself), either spoken or written; or if we see them, we cannot remember them afterward (so our present tense is relating a past experience), other than the single proclamation the man-clown writes in the snow: "I DID THIS!"

Words, language, are as writing in the snow. After his proclamation, the man collapses into hysterical laughter. We see that his smile is painted on, that he is, in fact, weeping. We leave him helpless as a beetle in the snow, then seem to see his face again for a moment. But it is actually the grin of death on the mouth of the white rabbit in the jaws of the dog whose hunt finally has succeeded. The last sound we hear is the crunching of the rabbit's bones followed once again by the "transcendent silence of winter."

Every approach here is made through the senses of hearing and seeing. Any interpretation is indirect but establishes a connection for later use. For example, our attention is called to the fact that we see only the surface of the snow and cannot know for sure the contours beneath it, foreshadowing our view beneath the smile of the man to his sadness. But we cannot hear the word he speaks over and over, "some terrible syllable." What might that syllable be? *Death* perhaps? For at once, the man's smile becomes the grimace of the dead rabbit.

Though a number of interpretative foci surely are possible, one can directly interpret the visual symbols imparted to the sensate lens of the reader: in the silence of the winter woods, death stalks life. A man steps off the "sleigh ride" of the mainstream. Like an artist, he attempts to make his mark in the perishable substance of existence; but language is futile to convey the single terrible syllable of death, and his attempts, little more than those of a clown, a failed entertainer, leave him helpless as a beetle. Finally, *he* is the life the hound of death has stalked. Bones grind between teeth until silence again reigns. Winter prevails.

The trick is that whether or not language is futile, this entire illusion has been produced by words and words only. Coover has succeeded where the man-clown failed. For look again: there is no dog, no rabbit, no man, no woods, no winter. There are only words on a page, in our mind, on the white silence of the blank page of the imminent "winter" (which Coover places in quotes in the title) of our death.

One thing more: both the language used and the scenes evoked by that language are beautiful and reflect the beauty of winter. As always, with Coover's fiction, though, where there is beauty, terror is never far behind.

"The Milkmaid of Salmaniego"

The second "Sentient Lens" story begins with the observation that there seems to be some "precise structure of predetermined images, both basic and prior to us, that describes [the milkmaid] to us before our senses have located her in the present combination of shapes and colors" (*P&D*, 175). Thus, we see her, Coover suggests; we become "aware of her undeniable approach" (*P&D*, 175). Coover, of course, is our lens here, or the only one privy to the lens, and he employs the first-person plural in referring to himself in that function.

In this way, he clues the reader in to what he is dealing with in this fiction, and how. The reader is admitted to Coover's aesthetic or imaginative process as he makes contact, so to speak, with "a precise structure of predetermined images, both basic and prior to us." Thus, the reader is with him as he recognizes his inspiration as an example of "unconscious mythic residue" against which he must struggle in order to combat the "exhausted art forms" and achieve "new complexities."[12]

"We might not on the other hand have thought of the man," he continues. The man, old and grotesque, sits by the bridge chewing bread with his yellow teeth, and his presence surprises "us" (that is, Coover's narrator) sufficiently to "encourage us to look for another bridge and another milkmaid, were such a happy option available" (*P&D*, 175).

He watches the milkmaid approach, the eggshell-white pitcher balanced on her head as though "for all time." "She moves with a gliding, *purely linear* motion down the dusty, rutted road" (*P&D*, 176, italics mine), looking neither right nor left.

Here the narrator-controlled fiction begins to pull toward the old man, but the narrator jerks it back: " . . . no, no! the maid, *the maid*!" (*P&D*, 176).

As "we" watch her, "we" (Coover's imagination in progress) "discover" that the pitcher is etched with fine "rust-colored veins" and is not a milk jug at all but a basket of fresh eggs on her head; as we watch they pop open and chicks tumble out around her feet. They flutter around her ankles and grow, transformed into hens, sows; soon she is surrounded by and feeding hens, sows, chickens, cattle with their calves, "glorifying in the happy milkmaid with the eggshell-white pitcher on her head" (*P&D*, 177). A young man appears, currying a bull. He attacks the maid, but she wrenches free, and the pitcher topples from her head, causing her to feel "a sudden lightening, almost a sense of growth." "The white liquid bubbles out of the narrow mouth, seeps futilely into the dry yellow dust of the rutted road" (*P&D*, 178). Apparently it is milk again. Or is it something else? The description could well be of the climax of an act of masturbation—the onanism of endlessly repeated convention. But she is relieved of this receptacle and, unburdened, feels herself grow.

With the spilling of the pitcher, all is suddenly gone—milk, eggs, animals, young man—she weeps. "Dry cracked hands" help her set the jug aright. Finally, she sees the old man. She is frightened, but he reassures her. The reader becomes aware of the long road she has traveled, the empty pitcher. What now remains for her? The old man draws from his pocket some gold and silver coins that look "like nothing less than a whole private universe of midsummer suns in the man's strong dark hand" (*P&D*, 179).

The pitcher tips off a ridge then and breaks into "a thousand tiny fragments not unlike the broken shells of white eggs" that tumble "into the eddying stream below" (*P&D*, 179).

The interpretation of a parable always has a clumsy feel to it, and that is one of the limitations of the form. Coover has constructed a parable here, but he rewards the reader with something more organic than a mere formula of symbols. The symbols he employs are carefully described images, living fragments of the mythic past. There is a reward for the reader in the evocative beauty of his writing—always an important element in Coover's short fiction—and in the way his images reach our own segment of the collective unconscious.

But more important, he invites us in as witnesses to the process of his own imagination, to which he himself is a spectator, though he undeniably guides us. On the question of balance between intellect and spontaneity in the writing of fiction, Coover has expressed his position thus: "Inner forces emerging from the narrative itself, whether as rebellious 'characters' or the 'spontaneous' eruption of event and imagery, are more to be trusted in the end than rational design, no matter how ingeniously contrived."[13]

Perhaps it is possible here to differentiate the details selected rationally (or as Wordsworth put it, "recollected in tranquility" following the spontaneous overflow) from those which appear of themselves, in spontaneous overflow. The maid's "linear" movement on the "dusty rutted road" seems clearly a consciously selected emblem of the conventional linear literature (mythic residue) that constitutes the path of least resistance to the writer. She carries on her head another emblem, the nourishing substances of creation—milk, eggs. A young man attacks her, spills the contents of the jug, and leaves her with nothing, but the old man appears to help her and show her the gold and silver of "a whole private universe of midsummer suns" (*not*, as in Gordon's quotation, "of mid*night* suns" [171]).

At one point in his writing Coover looked exclusively to the literature of four or more centuries past, finding contemporary work more distant and useless.[14] Thus, it might be reasonable to suggest that this parable is about the salvation of young writers—when they find the urn of inspiration empty—in the gold of the old masters.

"The Leper's Helix"

The last of the "Sentient Lens" fictions, "The Leper's Helix," is an eerie, abstract, yet sensually compelling (perhaps revolting is the better word) piece that Andersen suggests is intellectually stimulating but not human and therefore of "questionable" merit (36). Here again we meet the misconception that if fiction does not deal directly with human experience in a form that imitates it, then it is other than human. In other words, only realism is "human." But this argument forgets that realism is a mere tool with which to approach reality, or some aspect of reality, just as metafiction or surrealism are tools.

For in the mere space of three pages, Coover creates a remarkable experience that has undeniable power to touch the reader's sense of his reality or existence as a human being, even if it does not do so by directly imitating or evoking the emotions that come into play with normal human interchange.

In essence, this is a narration of the approach of a leper across a desert toward the narrator, following a pattern created by the narrator; as such it deals with what Cope refers to as "the inevitability of pattern" (3). The voice, reminiscent of a Poe narrator, observes the revolting creature approach, seen sometimes as a leper, sometimes as death, and plays with it. He observes it coolly, noting that its grotesque gait might even be comic under other circumstances, noting the eagerness and frustration of the approaching figure, whose arms flap like torn sails (*P&D*, 180).

The narrator's progress, on the other hand, is "precise, governed"; the approaching leper is observed from a superior position. But ultimately the mechanism set in motion runs its course, and when it does, the narrator is pained to realize that the moment of meeting has come, the pattern's inevitability is complete. "Had we thought, only *thought*, we could have drawn two circles, or ten circles, postponed this ultimate experience, but the choice was ours just once, our impulsive first action has become—alas!—a given, the inexorable governor of all that remains" (*P&D*, 181).

The narrator turns to greet the leper, to accept his horrific embrace. The leper dies in his arms, and *he* then becomes the leper, waiting for the reader to begin the game anew (*P&D*, 182). Thus the story ends as a continuum in which the reader, presumably, takes the place of the narrator and the narrator takes the place of the leper. The fiction itself, then, is that the leper embraces the reader, and once embraced, the reader is the leper, and so on, endlessly.

Our fiction is governed by the patterns we create for it, the patterns we accept for it. Through these patterns, the figure at the core of the pattern stalks us, like reality perhaps, like death, perhaps like Marianne Moore's real toads in imaginary gardens[15]—like whatever, after all, is genuine.

"A Pedestrian Accident"

"Paul stepped off the curb and got hit by a truck" is how this fiction begins (*P&D*, 183). The 22 pages that follow are a comic nightmare account of the remainder of his life.

Paul lies broken beneath the truck, experiencing déjà vu, wondering whether he is in the process of rebirth. The driver of the truck leans out of the cab to complain and justify himself while people gather and Paul wonders whether he crossed with the light. The faces around him are mostly reproachful or amused, a few are compassionate, a few jeering. "There were orations and the waving of flags" (*P&D*, 185). A policeman arrives, drives back the crowd, and questions Paul, who discovers he is incapable of speech.

The policeman grows impatient with him. A bawdy old woman in the crowd, reeking of gin, cries out that Paul is Amory Westerman, her lover, and rants on for several pages in various slapstick postures. All the while

Paul lies dying, thinking, "*I'm* the strange one" (*P&D*, 190). The policeman, seeking to restore order and quiet, shouts, "Can't you see this is a serious matter?" and Paul thinks, "He's the funny one" (*P&D*, 192). The old woman and the truck driver fight. She continues to disclaim. The policeman screams, "THIS IS ABSURD!" and Paul thinks, "You're warm . . . but that's not quite it" (*P&D*, 195).

The policeman continues to attempt to restore order and get help for Paul, but ineffectually. Finally, a doctor appears, occasioning more slapstick ("Thank God!" "I'd rather you credit the profession"). The doctor must have Paul out from beneath the truck to examine him, but since moving Paul could be dangerous, he demands that the truck back up over him—more slapstick. The driver moves the truck too far, so another set of wheels rolls up onto Paul's body. Newsmen take Paul's picture. "You'll be famous," one of them says, (*P&D*, 201), and, "His goddamn body is like mulligan stew," the doctor says. More slapstick follows. The doctor says to Paul, "Death begets life. . . . Survival and murder are synonymous, son, first flaw of the universe" (*P&D*, 202).

Paul dozes, wakes to see that printed on the side of the truck are the words, "MAGIC KISS LIPSTICK" (*P&D*, 204). Everyone is gone except for a derelict (whom Paul mistakes for a priest) waiting for him to die so he can take his clothes. A stray dog trots up and tears away a strip of Paul's flesh.

The street seems to upend, and for a moment Paul has a vision of himself hanging on it as though crucified; but he thinks, "There's nobody out there," and that vision vanishes. The piece ends with Paul waiting to die, wondering how much longer his torment must continue, and closes with his rhetorical repetition of the question, "How much longer?" (*P&D*, 205).

This is an unusually long and unevocative piece compared with the others in the book. Vaguely reminiscent of Edgar Allan Poe's "The Predicament" (1840), the piece is actually more like the Ole Olsen and Chic Johnson film *Hellzapoppin* (1941) than the existential nightmare parable it seems to wish to be. As in *Hellzapoppin*, slapstick follows absurd gag follows slapstick, until finally the belly wearies of laughing and the jokes begin to fall flat. The lengthy exchanges of slapstick dialogue (*P&D*, 187–96) in "A Pedestrian Accident" cease to amuse. All the characters, with the exception of Paul, have a clumsy cartoon texture to them, so that if it is an existential hell we see here, it is one that might have been conceived and drawn by Chester Gould. It is difficult to see this piece as anything more than a thin slice of dark entertainment, a meaningless burlesque with little more to recommend it than a laugh or two.

METHODIST COLLEGE LIBRARY
Fayetteville, N.C.

This is one fiction Coover might have weeded from the collection. Compared with some of the other early fictions, most of them much more concise and powerful, as well as with the other longer pieces, written after the breakthrough of "The Elevator"—masterpieces like "The Magic Poker" and "The Babysitter"—"A Pedestrian Accident" seems very much out of its class here.

Of course, Coover is a brilliant writer, and all his work bears at least some stamp of that brilliance. But here the brilliance seems more flash than substance, a piece of polished brass amid the golden midsummer suns in the artist's dark palm.

"The Babysitter"

Andersen finds this story technically fascinating but, again, lacking in human emotion and thus in literary merit (105). Such a postulation, however, can be based only on a narrow view of what constitutes meaningful human emotion and can only be informed, one suspects again, by a largely mimetic orientation to fiction.

"The Babysitter" certainly does deal with human emotion—with fear and delight, with idle desire and raw lust, and with the entire range of tamed yearnings that seethe beneath the narcotized surface of suburban life. The story enacts a flushing out of fear and of fictions ("mythic residue"), a turning of the suburban stone to reveal the teeming fictions of the quotidian. But these fears are far from hidden; they are not even restricted to the form of dream or wish or fantasy. If they start as such, they soon flare out into full-scale "behavior"—or do they? Everything happens at once here: civil behavior, lurid dream, soap-opera tragedy; acts of crime and passion in "life" and on TV exist side by side, separated only by inter-scene asterisks.

The whole circus of possibilities springs out as surely as Dolly Tucker's flesh when she slips down her girdle to answer nature's call and all the men at the feast are unable to get it back under constraint. The scenes shift as dizzyingly as the TV channels the eponymous babysitter keeps switching, and the sequence of the 107 unnumbered scenes is as jumbled as a William Burroughs chronology.

A babysitter comes to watch their three children while Dolly and Harry Tucker go to a Saturday evening party. The babysitter's boyfriend Jack and his friend Mark, who happens to be the son of the people giving the party the Tuckers go to, are shooting pinball and planing how to take advantage of Jack's girlfriend, the babysitter. Jack is not sure he likes this idea. But

Mark's personality is stronger, so Jack goes along with the plan, meanwhile fantasizing about beating Mark up and playing the hero before his girl-friend, all of which occurs in juxtaposition to a fistfight on the TV between a dark outlaw and the good sheriff. The babysitter is trying to get the two older kids bathed and in bed without waking the sleeping baby so she can avoid changing a dirty diaper, do her homework, and still have time to watch the Tuckers' good color TV set, although she would not mind having a visit from her boyfriend Jack either.

The kids, Jimmy and Bitsy, tease and tickle her while Harry Tucker, driving to the party, daydreams about sneaking back to try to seduce her and Dolly Tucker suffers in her too tight girdle. Jack and Mark's plans branch out to dreams of seducing her, to raping her, to spying on her in the bath, to spanking her, while little Jimmy pretends to have to use the bath-room to get to see her in the tub, and Bitsy evades her turn in the bath, throwing a pair of her father's underpants at the sitter, who in private can-not resist trying them on and examining the curious fly, whereupon Jack and Mark discover, in their scene, that she is wearing men's underpants, and little Jimmy sees the whole thing and threatens to tell.

Harry Tucker's fantasy, as he gets more and more drunk at the party, becomes increasingly compelling, and he plans to sneak back to get his glasses or aspirins or to check on the kids so he can be alone with the sitter. He becomes so drunk that he mutters fragments of his fantasy aloud, to the amusement of the others at the party and the annoyance of Dolly.

In a spiral of variations, Harry comes back and catches the sitter and Jack half undressed, throws Jack out, and takes advantage of the girl's situ-ation. Or he catches her in the tub alone and joins her. Or he finds her and the two boys peacefully watching the TV. Or he discovers, or *thinks* he dis-covers, the girl's underpants hung like a flag on the TV antenna. Or one of the boys notices that Harry has forgotten to close his fly and flatly calls the fact to his attention. Or little Jimmy sees the sitter in the tub, and she teas-ingly compels him to wash her back and fish around for the soap when he drops it in the bathwater. Or Jack and Mark catch her in the tub and acci-dentally drown her. Or Harry catches Jack, Mark, and the girl all in the tub, and then Dolly catches the four of them there. Or the baby wakes, the sitter has to change the soiled diaper, she gets stool on herself and Jimmy, they all have to take their clothes off, and she tries to wash the baby in the tub and drowns it. Or she sees a face at the window, or receives anonymous phone calls, or someone sneaks into the house and grabs her from behind. Or Harry Tucker spies through his own window, from the bushes, on the sitter while Dolly takes off her girdle in the host's bathroom and is unable to get it back on, and first the host and then the other guests all try to help squeeze her copious flesh back into it, using butter for lubrication. Harry sneaks out, comes back, and the sitter washes the dishes, does her homework, and none of this happens, or all of it happens. There is a report on the TV news about a babysitter who is killed, or it is another babysitter and the evening ends peacefully, an exemplary, suburban Saturday night. Or it all happens: the children are murdered, the husband disappears, there's a corpse in the bathtub, the house is wrecked, and Dolly's reaction is to see what is on the late late movie.

It all happens, none of it happens—107 variations of the fantasies, fears, anxieties, wish fulfillments, drunken blurs, crimes, sins, tragedies, and omissions of a suburban Saturday night—and it all ends with the note of discontent, of unfulfilled desire that has us look finally for one last diversion, the late late movie. An explosion of possibilities ends with a fizzle, a beehive comedy of everything and nothing, all going on before the flickering eye and changing channels of the TV.

The reality here is everything, the sum total of it all—that which happens, that which is only imagined, that which is watched, wished for, dreamed, planned, enacted, felt, and thought; a great internal-external spiral, half-real/half-imagined, is certainly not realism, but the reality that realism conceals in the interest of literary convention.

"The Hat Act"

"The Hat Act" is a fitting finale to Coover's brilliant fictions collected in *P&D*. Like Coover, who has surprised, awed, baffled, astonished, entertained, sometimes for a moment or two bored, delighted, and titillated the reader with piece after piece, so too the magician who is the main character in "The Hat Act"; he plays to an audience whose response, like that of a reader, must be earned and is never extended free of charge. (After all, they have paid to be entertained, and Coover is not playing to a closed audience of academics; he is out in the commercial mainstream, technically and literarily refined as he is.)

The audience will accept a traditional trick or two and will applaud the conjuring, from the hat, of a dove, a rabbit; but as the tricks are repeated, even in surprising variations, the laughter and clapping fall away and are replaced by hissing and booing. The magician is ahead of them, however: his magic becomes increasingly facile and astonishing, as he skirts the edge of danger, of mortality. The tricks begin to seem no mere sleight-of-hand or illusion but true magic, crossing the borders of natural law, plunging beyond the limits of what mortal man can do.

He disappears into his own hat, reappears, calls for volunteers to rip his head from his body, and reappears out of his own fly. The audience members no longer merely applaud or whistle; now they shriek and scream until the magician releases them from terror to resolve his tricks, which become increasingly brutal and unconcerned with the people called upon to assist him.

Finally, things run out of control. He is unable to undo one of his illusions and in frustration brutally kills his assistant. He is bound and led off the stage, to the weeping and moaning of the audience, while a sign is hung out, "THIS ACT IS CONCLUDED. THE MANAGEMENT REGRETS THERE WILL BE NO REFUND" (*P&D*, 256). These concluding words of the book are appropriately amusing and ironic.

Like a magician, a fiction writer is an illusionist. But the "true" magician involves himself in more than sleight-of-hand, just as the "true" artist seeks to deal profoundly with reality rather than merely entertain. The tool is the same. Both magician and writer work with the imagination, an orderly intentional mental process, the creative faculty of the human mind, the formative power. Unlike angels, who are mere messengers, exalted though they may be, man can create. Magicians, however, deal not only with the creative forces of the universe but with the destructive forces. In their efforts to achieve mastery over their lives, men who seek to practice the art of magic deal with elements of the imagination and the will.

In the words of the nineteenth-century magician Eliphas Levy, "To know, to dare, to will, to keep silence . . . such are the four words of the Magus"[16]—words not unlike the names of the "arms" Joyce declared for himself as a writer: "silence, exile, and cunning."[17] Perhaps the most famous magician of this century, Aleister Crowley (1875–1947), was also a poet, and many writers are known to have involved themselves in cults of magic, including the Nobel laureate W. B. Yeats, who was a member of the Order of the Golden Dawn, of which Crowley was also a member.

Some magicians go very far in the pursuit of their craft; Crowley, who relished being referred to as "The Great Beast" (the beast prophesied in Revelations), is rumored to have been involved in a rite that resulted in the murder of a child. Some writers, as suggested by R. H. W. Dillard, deal with "the power of the imagination and its inextricable involvement with religion and sexual urgings" and with the danger inherent in this.[18]

Dillard suggests that Coover has learned about

> the danger of the freed imagination, a lesson that Blake knew and that Poe
> and Melville, Kafka, Borges and Nabokov were to repeat for those who
> would hear. The murderous and idealistic narrator of "Ligeia," mad Ahab,
> caught K, Humbert Humbert and Kinbote dreaming of an immortality akin to
> that of Yeats' golden bird—these are the victims and villains of the freed
> imagination, destroyed by a perversion of the very force of life as brutal and
> as thorough as cancer. Coover knows that lesson well and the cure; in these
> fictions, he journeys toward the New World, but he is ever mindful both that
> the nag is a bag of bones and that the New World may prove to be a night-
> mare without the necessary love and craft essential to life and art. The imagi-
> nation is always eager to enter the world, to people it with its own creations
> which, like those of nature, proliferate with fantastic abandon. The artist, as
> the type of the imaginative man, must control the combinations tumbling in
> his mind, yearning for the life of the world. The imagination is continually
> getting out of hand in these stories—not Coover's, but his characters'.

Thus, excellent as it may otherwise be, Andersen's evaluation of "The
Hat Act" comes close but misses the mark when he says, "Exploring the
technical possibilities available in fiction and the new perspectives of literature and life that they provide, Coover focuses most of his attention on
what is magic rather than what is human in art." Andersen concludes,
"Coover's fictions amount to little more than fascinating but impersonal
mental exercises that might very well inspire some readers to request a
refund" (107).

Here, again, I think it is important to underscore the necessity of not
approaching Coover with an insistence on mimesis. Surely Coover uses the
tools of mimesis and of realism with brilliance, but the reality he is dealing
with goes beyond the surface of quotidian realism, and the qualities of
humanity he touches are indeed very human, quintessentially so.

Coover is dealing with our power to create ourselves, to imagine ourselves. His "Hat Act" is far more than a technical trick; it is a parable of the
dangers of this powerful existential tool of our imagination. In Gordon
Weaver's metafiction "The Parts of Speech" (1986) the narrator speculates
as to whether the motives behind the fiction-making process are a "wholly
good thing."[19] In "The Hat Act" we witness a running wild of the imagination that results in death and destruction, and the commercial promoters of
art quickly issue a disclaimer of nonresponsibility: no refunds. Still, Coover
does not allow his parable to run so far that it chokes on its own repercus-
sions. Always beneath the surface is just the necessary measure of dis-

tancing irony, of dark humor that will keep us from taking it so seriously that the point is lost. What more amusing way for an author to conclude a book than to tell the reader, "I'm sorry, you can't get your money back."

And in truth, who could request a refund after the circus of astonishments of this collection? For the price of a book, the reader is led through halls of the imagination from which he will emerge into a New World of fiction. The original dust jacket of *Pricksongs & Descants* bore this statement from Coover: "I offer these apprentice calculations . . . begging . . . to remember the Wisdom of the Beast: 'If I carry the poison in my head, in my tail which I bite with rage lies the remedy.' "

Pricksongs & Descants is a work of true genius, a remedy for the dead end of convention, a book that on its own ought to guarantee a permanent place for Coover in American letters.

In Bed One Night &
Other Brief Encounters

This collection was issued in a limited edition of 1200 copies by Burning Deck Press in 1983.[1] It contains nine pieces, mostly miniatures, that were originally published during the 1970s in a variety of journals and magazines, from *Oink!* to *Harper's*. It is gratifying to note, in this time of Jesse Helms, the author's acknowledgment to the National Endowment for the Arts, which today might have reservations about funding a writer whose expression is as free as Coover's.

Although the pieces are described as fictions on the acknowledgments page, a case might be made for classifying a number of them as poems or prose poems or proems, or perhaps as simply metafictional exercises. Of Coover's three collections, this is clearly the lightest and, at 59 pages, the *slightest*, though it still bears the unmistakable, undeniable stamp of his genius and originality. There are elements of Russel Edson as well as of *Les Pensées* in these meditation pieces on the nature of language and art, as well as in the one full-blown, if flawed, metafiction that provokes thought and delight and is peppered with one-liners to engage the mind and tickle the belly.

"The Debris"

The collection opens with "The Debris," which I would call a poem, or proem, about memory and remembrance and the useless dead we carry with us, the things we yearn to remember and cannot.[2] A man on a moonlit beach discovers the body of a dead woman. As he tries to recall a forgotten memory, he wonders what to make of her—a metaphor for dead conventions perhaps.

"The Old Man"

"The Old Man" is a poem about an unwanted, unseen old man who feeds the birds.[3] They teach him to fly so he can "show" all those who disregard him, but he is frightened by the height, and we leave him begging the birds to get him down again.

"In Bed One Night"

"In Bed One Night" is a satirical sociological fiction (and little surprise it appeared originally in *Playboy*) about a world in which "private beds are a luxury the world can no longer afford" (*IBON*, 15).[4] A man gets into his bed one night to find it full of strangers sent there by the social security authorities.

"Getting to Wichita"

"Getting to Wichita" is a prose poem about a man who drives into a filling station to ask directions to Wichita. The mechanic mouths useless philosophical replies at him until he finally makes a purchase, and then communication seems to kick into gear. There would seem to be a statement here, though a more blatant one than we are accustomed to from Coover.

"The Tinkerer"

"The Tinkerer" is a clever piece about a man who takes a chance and invents "mind."[5] It seems not to work as well as other inventions ("heart appetite the city") so he thinks of starting over with something new ("melody or force"), following the old rule of "work with what you know" (the classic advice to the young writer) (*IBON*, 23). Mind captures his imagination nonetheless, so he waits for it to run down and makes a few adjustments, "hoping for the best or at least a brief entertainment," but now mind runs completely amok (*IBON*, 23). He realizes that he actually invented not mind but love, and now he's blown it. He tries to get hold of his invention to make it back into what it was, but it wreaks havoc on the world, which promptly turns angrily upon the inventor. He flees underground, fearing it is only a matter of time before either the city fathers or his invention gets him, but he goes on anyway "frantically inventing serenity" and dreaming of a world free of "the menace of misbegotten thingamagigs" (*IBON*, 25).

"The Fallguy's Faith"

"The Fallguy's Faith" starts as an extended wordplay on the varied idiomatic uses of the word *fall*.[6] A character makes all the falls a person can experience, both physically, through time and space, and figuratively, from favor, grace, short of expectation, into bad habits, out with friends, in and out of love, foul of the law, and so on. But the play soon thickens: "Why was it that everything that happened to him seemed to have happened in language? . . . Almost as though without words for it, it might not have happened at all!" (*IBON*, 27). The character becomes aware that he is nothing but words, and he also realizes, as he is falling and dying, that it could be said he has been born to fall and thus fallen to be born. But even as he opens his mouth to speak his understanding, the words die on his lips. "The Fallguy's Faith" is a memorable piece about the function of language in creating the meaning of experience and, by metafictional parallel, about how language patterns predetermine the meaning of our experience. Meaning is "born" of words to fulfill an idiom as surely as a character in a fiction is "born" to fulfill the destiny of the fiction.

"An Encounter"

"An Encounter" is the "story" of a character who, moving from empty room to empty room, recognizes he is having an encounter with emptiness through empty room after empty room after empty room.[7] The first excitement of his recognition, however, begins to pale, and the encounter becomes less interesting for him, every room the same, the same, but then he recognizes he is having an encounter with sameness, and the recognition makes him feel better. But soon he sees that sameness is not as good as emptiness. He tries stopping, but stopping is not good, it's worse. So he begins to run from room to room, but that is no good either, and he wonders where it will end, until "a door closed and he"—which concludes the piece, another amusing play on the nature of language as the creator of meaning and the limited pleasures of existential *huis clos.*

"The Convention"

"The Convention" is an unpunctuated flow of broken prose that follows Tom's increasingly frantic progress through a "convention" hotel where all the conventional convention clichés of booze, broads, and lewd buffoons move faster and faster and story lines intermingle as jokes blend with "reality": the activities on different floors, in different rooms, all running together, sour bartenders, aggressive prostitutes, gag nametags, prostitutes, barroom folk tales of strippers and Danish sex, "important things," big cigars, back slaps, fistfights, and men roaming the hotel drinking and looking for women: "hell its what conventions are all about" (*IBON*, 39).[8]

In response to my request to run an excerpt from "The Convention" as a sidebar to my interview with him (1991), Robert Coover said that would be "like excerpting a sneeze."[9] It is, however, one of the longer pieces in this collection, and one that, with two others, is undeniably fiction. Amusing as the piece may be, however, its aim seems more low than high. It is an extended, well-told, slapstick gag, poking fun at the stock picture of the American convention as literary convention.

"Beginnings"

Appropriately enough, the collection ends with a piece entitled "Beginnings," which itself begins with an ending and ends with a beginning.[10] "Beginnings" is a brilliantly funny, if flawed, second cousin to "The Magic Poker"; it is a piece one might imagine Coover having sorted out of the short list of pieces finally selected for *P&D*.

Andersen sees Coover's story as a sort of unconcluded "constant middle," an "open-ended challenge to his readers' imaginations" (99). But it might equally be viewed as a metaphorically straightforward, if somewhat cubistic, metafictional representation of a writer's block, a writer's futile retreat to an island to get started on a new work only to find himself knee-deep in unworkable ideas and crumbs of first sentences.

The piece begins: "In order to get started, he went to live alone on an island and shot himself. His blood, unable to resist a final joke, splattered the cabin wall in a pattern that read: It is important to begin when everything is already over" (*IBON*, 40). Throughout the piece the writer periodically blows his brains out again, "like taking a cathartic" (*IBON*, 47) (echoes of the wisdom of the beast whose poison is in his mind).

Soon, however, the character is no longer alone. He is joined by Eve, who claims to be the original inhabitant of the island, a claim she proves by showing him her missing rib, whereupon he returns the rib, discovering "it is more blessed to give than receive." They decide to call this exchange "fucking" (*IBON*, 45) and spend a great deal of time repeating it.

Where previously he had company only when he desired to visit people a mile's boat-ride away ("they often told him stories, astounding him with their fearless capacity for denouement" [*IBON*, 41]), Eve produces many babies (some of whom he eats, though he always regrets it, as they constipate him) and disturbs his solitude, assigning him chores and tempting him to sex. He continues to blow out his brains regularly and tries new stories, variations of Bible tales, myths, apocalypses, "phrases lying about like stones, metaphors growing like stunted bushes" (*IBON*, 57). "First lines lay about like fallen trees," or, he awakes in the morning "tangled in first lines like wrinkled sheets" (*IBON*, 58).

Finally, he sees that it is time to leave the island and make a fresh start. As they sail away, the island sinks ("You did that on purpose, the woman said" [*IBON*, 58]).

The piece concludes: "So much for fresh starts. He might as well not have pulled the trigger in the first place. But it was done and that was an end to it. Or so it said on the cabin wall" (*IBON*, 59).

The story is studded with brilliant one-liners but flawed with jokes that fall flat: Eve uses his typewriter ribbon as a clothesline to hang diapers on; he uses manuscript sheets in lieu of bread for peanut butter sandwiches. "Beginnings" suffers finally from a nearsightedness of vision compared with its more fully developed cousin "The Magic Poker." It was perhaps a forestudy or the after-leavings of the more complete and satisfying pieces of *Pricksongs & Descants*.

Still, it is a Coover, a well-wrought and memorable piece of metafiction, a fitting conclusion to this little book of miniatures.

A Night at the Movies or, You Must Remember This

The thematic and metaphorical coherence of *A Night at the Movies* gives it a unity not often seen in a short story collection. Cope goes so far as to call the book "a novel plotted on the experience of attending that range of continuity enveloping discontinuity which used to constitute an actual night spent at the movies" (136). If it is a novel, however, it is not one in any strict sense, and since a number of its components have previously appeared on their own—several years before the publication of the collection in 1987—and stand well on their own, it does seem more appropriate to view the work as a collection of fictions on the related "cinematic" themes of nostalgia, memory, the pursuit of identity in metaphor, and the function of film for contemporary American society.[1]

Film is experience safely captured as surely as the experience which we survive to encapsulate as memory. Apart from the discovery of new facts, nothing new can happen to disrupt the known contours of what is safely in the past, what is "complete," so to speak, just as nothing can change the sequence of a film in the can. Or can it?

"The Phantom of the Movie Palace"

This opening to the collection seems to play on the static nature of "completed" film, merging cinematic scene and known films into a composite experience in a fiction whose universe consists of a projectionist, a theater, a screen, and seemingly all the films ever made up to about 1950.

"The Phantom" opens with a series of parodies of film genres and stereotypes—science fiction, gangster film, "the handsome young priest with boyish smile" (though here crooning to a man in the next toilet stall) (*ANM*, 14), horror, "a man with an axe in his forehead" panicking a movie audience which begins to blend and change places with the film (15) in the way that B-movies and television thrillers occasionally make heavy-handed use of metafilm strategy.

The point of view shifts to the projectionist "changing reels in his empty palace" (*ANM*, 15), yearning for the past. He "keeps" the theater, cleaning and sweeping it daily, although there is no one to clean up after and no one comes to his palace anymore. No sooner does the projectionist appear than the fiction slides off into yet another film composite: a legionnaire lost in the desert climbs aboard a sinking luxury liner. Mischievous children plan to stick a hornet's nest in the truant officer's pants. An orphan girl is crawling up a ladder to the hayloft where "some cruel fate awaits her," suggested by a close-up of the holes in her underwear—or are they water spots on the old film? The projectionist stops the movie for a closer look, but the aged film is "forever blurred, forever enigmatic." "There's always this unbridgeable distance between the eye and its object" (*ANM*, 17).

Meaning itself seems to pursue both the images on the screen and the projectionist. He wanders the opulent old movie palace, turning on lights, floodlights, and the popcorn machine, and explores its secret rooms and subterranean tunnels where, it is said, there is access to "even deeper levels ... linkages to all the underground burrowings of the city." But "dark anxiety ... drives him back up into the well-lit rooms above ... to the homely comforts of his little projection booth" (*ANM*, 19).

He switches lights off "as he goes, dragging darkness behind him like a fluttering cape" (*ANM*, 20), while the cat woman seduces the hayseed superhero and the ingenue sings her only line again and again—"Love!" in a film packed with matings and battle. The high priestess comes on to the ape man, who can think of little else but to call for his elephants (*ANM*, 21).

The projectionist experiments, superimposing films upon one another, crossing them; he assaults "a favorite ingenue ... with a thick impasto of pirates, sailors, bandits, gypsies, mummies, Nazis, vampires, Martians, and college boys, until the terrified expressions on their respective faces pale to a kind of blurred, mystical affirmation of the universe" (*ANM*, 22).

Or he turns off the projector lights and fills the theater with the sound of "blobs and ghouls, robots, galloping hooves and screeching tires, creaking doors, screams, gasps of pleasure and fear" (*ANM*, 22).

Some of the stratagems he invents himself; others come to him by accident. Films stick together, and images transpose. He drives stampedes through upper-story hotel rooms, beards a breast, clothes a hurricane in a tutu. "He knows there is something corrupt, maybe even dangerous, about this collapsing of boundaries, but it is so liberating ... and it is also necessary" (*ANM*, 23).

The projectionist understands that the crisis the film characters are made to suffer in this way "is merely the elemental crisis in his own heart"

(*ANM,* 24). Image follows image for pages of collage and juxtaposition. "He recognizes in all these dislocations . . . his lonely quest for the impossible mating, the crazy embrace of polarities, as though the distance between the terror and the comedy of the void were somehow erotic—it's a kind of pornography." He continues, image upon image upon image, "just to prove to himself over and over again that nothing and everything is true" (*ANM,* 25).

His experiments proceed, become more daring, ingenious, dangerous. He turns two projectors on their sides, causing the image and gravity of two separate worlds to intermingle, but something happens. He seems to have lost the ingenue. Has she fallen from the film? Escaped perhaps? He feels the pain of his loneliness—perhaps she is out there in the movie house itself? He leaves his projection room to look for her and finds these words cut into the movie screen: "Beware the Midnight Man!" (*ANM,* 29)

Light and images flare through the theater. He flees back to the projection room but is blocked by "thickets of tangled film spooling out at him like some monstrous birth." He cuts through but finds his projectors are gone. "It's as though his mind has got outside itself somehow, leaving his skull full of empty room presence." But "she" has been there and written a message in lipstick: "FIRST THE HUNT, THEN THE REVELS!" (*ANM,* 31).

Tentacles of film seem to be trying to strangle him. He flees again and throws the light switches, but nothing happens. "The ingenue's insane giggle rattles hollowly through the darkened palace" (*ANM,* 31). He continues through the menagerie of film images, though his objective is unclear. The prose becomes Chandlerian (as he falls 30 feet down the grand foyer wall: "It's a long way back down, but he gets there right away" [*ANM,* 33]), and then, as he wanders into a *Casablanca*-like scene, mock-Chandlerian, à la, say, Bob Hope in a haunted house ("There's a cold metallic hand in his pants. He screams. Then he realizes it's his own" [*ANM,* 34]).

But in fact, he is still lying curled up on the floor after his fall, though now in the middle of an 18th century ballroom, people minuetting around him while musketfire sounds from the streets (34). He looks up and sees the ingenue on the mirrored ceiling. The ballroom tips, and all the film images slide out into the public square, "where the terror nets them like flopping fish." "He is pulled to his feet and prodded into line between a drunken countess and an animated pig" (*ANM,* 35), then marched along the thickly carpeted aisle to the guillotine which is "rising and dropping like a link-and-claw mechanism" (*ANM,* 36).

The projectionist looks for the exit and protests that he does not belong there; the drunken countess tells him it is "the vages [wages] of cinema"

(*ANM*, 36). "It's all in your mind," says an usherette, pointing the way to the guillotine with her flashlight, "so we're cutting it off." As he is positioned and the blade drops, he finds himself "recalling a film he once saw (*The Revenge of Something-or-Other*, or *The Return of, The Curse of . . .*), in which—" (*ANM*, 36).

Cope points to the importance of the link-and-claw imagery that runs through the story—the mechanics of the projector, the machine that sends forth the images (137–38). Machine and man, projector and projectionist, make up a solipsistic universe in which all activity consists of finding metaphors for "the elemental crisis in his [the projectionist's] own heart . . . a lonely quest for the impossible mating, this crazy embrace of polarities . . . the terror and comedy of the void." (The link-and-claw "theory" will appear again in the pages to follow.)

And in the end, as with the hero of Barth's *Lost in the Funhouse* (1968), the projectionist's existence mixes with the films, is lost in the films, and *becomes* the metaphor for himself, losing his head. Finally it is all in his mind, and the only way out is to cut it off, the irony presumably being that loss of mind is a continuance of mindless activity, the projectionist's empty and solipsistic pursuit of nostalgia and metaphor even as meaning pursues—and eludes—him.

After Lazarus

In *After Lazarus*[2] language pretends to be film in much the manner of *P&D*'s "The Sentient Lens"—"Scene for 'Winter.'"

Starting with titles and credits and a hollow voice repeatedly crying "I have risen!" the narrative fills in background by describing camera angles, light, shadow. The camera follows the main street of clay houses. "No trees, grass, flowers; no animals; everything is empty and silent. The doors are all closed, the windows shuttered. Long steady contemplative takes" (*ANM*, 37). In the background, unfocused, is a cathedral. The camera moves into the side streets and becomes increasingly unsteady. The searching camera begins to follow an old woman down the rutted street (*ANM*, 39) to the cathedral (*ANM*, 40).

There is funeral music, a priest, a procession of gaunt men—their faces identical with that of the priest—and 12 pallbearers also "duplicates of the priest" (*ANM*, 41). Behind the coffin come the mourners, all women; dust rises but does not dull the glitter of their hard-polished shoes. The camera rises to the face of the dead man in the casket, also identical to the others (*ANM*, 42). The road is lined with mourners dressed in black, hundreds of them, all with the same face as the priest. The procession proceeds to the cemetery, where pictures of all the dead also reflect the same face and where "weeds, flowers, grass grow wildly" (*ANM*, 43). The camera stops at an open grave, and the pallbearers lower the casket in. "Suddenly the hands of the corpse lift tremblingly from his chest" (*ANM*, 44).

The resurrected corpse crawls out of the grave. A pallbearer flings him back in. There is a community wail, then silence, and the pallbearer is all alone in the cemetery. The road to the village too is desolate (*ANM*, 45). He runs back to the village, followed by the camera. It, too, is empty.

Again the hollow voice is heard: "I have risen!" The pallbearer returns to the house from within which is heard the sound of a heartbeat. He rushes inside. There is a black dress and shawl on a chair; the pallbearer hurriedly pulls on these clothes and looks up to see himself—"the pallbearer standing before her" (*ANM*, 46). He goes into the next house and repeats these actions while the heartbeat continues. There is a succession of pallbearers, a succession of dresses and shawls, a succession of heartbeats. The pallbearer produces from "her" skirts further dresses and shawls, undoes his fly and produces yet another shawl and dress. A similar succession of tricks occur with a white flower.

The pallbearer runs out into the street, follows the sound of the funeral music, bounds into the cathedral, finds the robes of the priest, pulls them on, orders another pallbearer to don the robes of the assistant, who in turn orders another pallbearer to don the robes of a lesser assistant, and so on. The procession begins again while the pallbearer watches from the cathedral doors. Then he stumbles down the steps, joins the procession, and climbs into the casket. The pallbearers proceed to the cemetery and lower the casket "toward the camera" into the grave. Darkness is followed by silence, a scraping sound like that of mice in a wall, then silence again, with which the piece concludes (*ANM*, 52) .

It is interesting to note that *After Lazarus* is devoid of prophets or religious analogies and has none but the very faintest of similarities to the story of Lazarus told in John (11:1–44), which has provided so many proverbs in our literature—including, inter alia, Kierkegaard's famous "sickness unto death" (11:4) and the often quoted, sometimes ironically, "Jesus wept" (11:35). There is no Jesus here, no Martha, no Mary, no Thomas, no Lazarus even, nor any sign of the necromantic act that finally inspires Caiaphas to begin plotting Jesus' death (11:53). There is only a village of like-faced people, a funeral procession, a corpse that crawls out of the grave only to be flung back by a pallbearer—a rejected resurrection, so to speak—who will ultimately change roles with the priest and the corpse in a reenactment of the apparently continuing ritual of funeral, "resurrection," and rejection of resurrection, a series of role changes and reenactments.

Why?

There are many layers of meaning to John's brief account of the raising of Lazarus—the humanity of Christ; indications of the dual purpose of his role as savior of the nation and of the individual; a dramatic element foreshadowing his threat to the existing order; and that order's crafty response. But the meaning of Coover's resurrection story seems more elusive.

I note that both Cope and Andersen say little or nothing about this piece, while Gordon goes on at some length (7, 10, 87, 89, 159–61). But ultimately she sheds little light on this cryptic mock filmscript of a fiction other than to conclude, "[T]he variety of one's associations with this filmscript will depend, as ever, upon his literary and psychological history. . . . [T]he appeal of the work is clearly more emotional than rational . . . a poetic transcription of archetypal dream landscapes" (160–61).

It would be difficult to deny the grain of truth in such sweeping statements, but I find myself hard-pressed to provide a cogent interpretation of this fiction. Certainly, there are intriguing elements in it as well as repeated details that tantalize with apparent significance (the polished shoes of the women, the scraping sound like mice in the wall—scratchings from the grave? or the sound of the movie projector?). But what is the ultimate *experience* of the piece?

Are we witnessing the triumph of ritual over substance? Of costume and role over identity? Why indeed does the pallbearer fling the resurrected corpse back into the grave and run for his life? Why do all others disappear at that moment? Why does everyone have the same face? Why are we made witness to the long train of cross-dressings until the pallbearer finally finds a costume that unites his identity in the priest (the unity of male and female perhaps)? And why does he only then proceed to take on the role of the corpse? And is he "dead"? Was the original corpse dead before it climbed out of the coffin? Is it suggestive that this *formally* filmic tale of rejected resurrection follows a tale of execution ("The Phantom of the Movie Palace") that is filmic in *content*? Does its superior title (which appears above the title) on the book's contents page, "Weekly Serial," "mean" something, or is it there purely for effect? Are we to make assumptions about the streets being without vegetation while the graveyard abounds with wild growth (perhaps calling to mind Wallace Stevens's "The vegetation abounds with forms")?

Or are these literal inspections of detail irrelevant here? Are we indeed merely witnessing an emotional, irrational exercise, a series of "archetypal dream images," a psycho-literary mirror designed only to evoke a response from our own literary and psychological histories?

Unlike Coover's other biblical stories, "J's Marriage" and "The Brother," *After Lazarus* is almost completely devoid of human psychology, but I do not see here the sharp metafictional elements one finds in his other "nonhuman" stories, such as "The Hat Act" or "The Leper's Helix." The images we are shown *are* dreamlike, perhaps archetypal, and like a dream they do certainly intrigue.

"Shootout at Gentry's Junction"

"Shootout at Gentry's Junction" is the western adventure portion of our *Night at the Movies*, a takeoff, inter alia, on *High Noon* (1952) and a multitude of other films before and since.[3]

Sheriff Henry "Hank" Harmon is waiting for the treacherous Mex to arrive in Gentry's Junction on the 12:10 (or possibly before—for some reason that number sticks in his head). Meanwhile, the Mex is in the saloon entertaining the locals with tales of the "womans." Shift back to Hank walking the streets of the town searching for the Mex. The streets are deserted. The town has left him to do what he has to do on his own, as always.

Back to the Mex, who is in the sheriff's office, crumbling cow chips into the humidor and penciling an obscene portrait of himself onto a picture of the sheriff's Belle. He sets fire to the sheriff's papers and, laughing, urinates on them while from the street come the sounds of a gathering festival.

Meanwhile, the sheriff is in the saloon trying to recruit men to help him face the Mex. Although he knows they won't help, that in the end he will have to do it alone, he has to give them the chance so that afterward they can feel guilt. "If they couldn't be heroes, they anyway had to learn to be men" (*ANM*, 55). He tells them he will return to the saloon in 15 minutes and expects them all to be there wearing their guns.

Shift to the Mex, who is in the bar tormenting an old man whose wife has died during the night. "Eh amigo! Why you no laugh, eh? We all happy here!" (*ANM*, 58). With his "soft brown fingers," he forces the old man's weeping face into a smile and then laughs and everyone in the saloon laughs with him. People seem unable to resist joining in with his laughter, though there may be some hatred and resentment beneath it.

The sheriff rides out to the edge of town to the big ranch of the banker, Gentry, who is cowering behind his bedroom door. Hank orders the banker to join him; the cowering Gentry tries in vain with an envelope full of cash to bribe Hank, who preaches to the banker about the decay of law and order that has come to the town with the Mex. Hank gruffly orders the cowardly banker to tie on his gun and be at Flem's Store in 15 minutes. Then he rides off.

Meanwhile the Mex is everywhere, burning and stealing and derailing "the foolish trains." He "finds great pleasure in the life. He is never never sad" (*ANM*, 61). He corrupts the schoolchildren and gags and binds and rapes the schoolmarm for their entertainment, eating her apple while he does so. The children love him. Or he is in the saloon gambling, holding five aces against Señor Gentry, who has just lost his wife, his mother, and three of his female children. Gentry tries to warn the Mex about the sheriff's intentions, but the Mex only laughs and breaks wind, a talent for which he is legendary.

The sheriff visits the church and debates good and evil with the preacher who is perhaps hiding his cowardice behind his fear. Hank orders him to be at Flem's Store at noon to witness, to show which side God is on. The preacher, learning that it is not necessary for him to be armed, reluctantly agrees.

The Mex again is everywhere, trying to satisfy his insatiable thirst, hunger, and greed, exercising the powers of his legendary bowels.

The sheriff stops in the hotel to see his Belle (who lives in room 1210) and arrives just in time to hear the obscene laughter of the departing Mex, who has raped her and left her feeling apparently ambivalent about the experience. But the sheriff's judgmental presence makes her turn against the Mex.

At Flem's Store, Hank meets the cowardly banker and the preacher and Flem. He will disarm the Mex, and they are to help tie the outlaw up so they can wait for the stagecoach with the judge and the marshall. Meanwhile, the little fat Mex is robbing the stagecoach, raping the judge's daughter, and kidnapping the marshall's wife.

The sheriff goes to the saloon to find it empty. He must face the Mex alone. He walks alone down the dusty Main Street, spurs jingling, dust puffing up from his boot heels.

The Mex is sitting on an upturned bucket on the street beneath the noon sun, chewing a toothpick, holding a watch. He offers the sheriff the watch (the sheriff's own). It is 12:09. The sheriff disarms the Mex, finds his weapons old and rusty, signals for the others to come out with the rope to tie up this fraud of a bandit, smells something foul, hears a click, goes for his gun, finds an empty holster, turns to see the Mex holding his own pistol, and receives "a silver bullet from his own gun square in his handsome suntanned face" (*ANM*, 72).

The Mex rides off on his pinto into the setting sun, leaving the town in flames behind him, the shopkeeper, the banker, and the preacher swinging "with soft felicity" from scaffolds, while the whiskey runs like blood, "the womans" scream merrily, and "Red red gleams the little five-pointed star [which he has stolen from the sheriff] in the ultimate light of the western sun" (*ANM*, 73).

This story hardly needs to be interpreted. It is a parody, a satire of the classic western film plot embodying the core myth of popular American culture: the triumph of law over chaos, of courage over cowardice, of good over evil. As with any satire, however, the familiar is reversed. "Evil" triumphs and leaves behind a scene reminiscent in theme of one Carl Jung recalls in his memoirs of his youth: When he looked at the Cathedral of Bern as a child, he felt his mind lock each time he gazed upon its lofty golden roof, and a terrible anxiety would grip him. Finally, in bed one night, he closed his eyes and opened his mind to the image that so insistently wished to appear: a great turd falling from the heavens and smashing the pristine roof of the cathedral.[4] This act of the imagination apparently helped the boy Jung to reintegrate the "high" and "low" elements of existence. This also seems to be one of Coover's main intentions—again, the beast with poisoned brain chewing at its tail.

"Selected Short Subjects"

"Gilda's Dream"
"Gilda's Dream," the first of the three "Selected Short Subjects," is certainly short—a single page. Within this context, the title evokes the 1940s film *Gilda*, in which Rita Hayworth performs a provocative dance in a South American nightclub; but in Coover's first-person "Gilda," the dance is a male striptease performed in a men's room in a foreign country where many languages are being spoken.

"What was odd about it ... was that I had started from the bottom up, so to speak, planning to ease myself to the top, but my face remained covered." The dancer sings "Put the Blame on the Dames." The toilet attendant, "pointing at my oddly numbered testicles," calls him a peasant (*ANM*, 74).

"Nothing was clear except for the danger I was in. I was breaking into little pieces, and not all of them seemed to be my own." A man is watching him through the louvered door of a stall. "I knew he was watching me . . . because I could see myself through his eyes" (*ANM*, 75).

From that perspective, he realizes that he is both threatening and desirable, that the fear in the room belongs to the room rather than himself. This realization makes him feel liberated, and he fires the attendant, shoots the Germans, tosses his head, and removes a glove, feeling himself back together again. But he hears the click of "the secret weapon" and realizes he has gambled and lost: "My pride, my penis, my glove, my enigmatic beauty, my good name, everything. There would be no going home" (*ANM*, 75).

Cope identifies "the click of the secret weapon" with the link-and-claw of the projector (143)—as good a guess as any. But Cope goes no further to explain the function of the image or why it leads to the narrator's realization that he has lost his gamble, or what precisely the gamble is.

Presumably the piece is an imagined dream in the mind of a character in an actual film; as such, it functions well as a blend of dream and film myth. It also functions as a reversal of myth, though less literally than "The Shootout at Gentry's Junction." Here, nevertheless, the reversal is complete—from temple dance to men's room transvestism.

"Inside the Frame"
The next "selected short," "Inside the Frame," is a bit longer and packed tight with one filmic metaphor after another—tumbleweeds, a banging screen door, a shoot-out, a rich woman with a "Negro" servant, a springing Indian with a knife between his teeth—interlaced with surreal images, such as a riderless horse in the distance, or a dog with a broken back. As in the preceding short, the language of film is crossed with dream: a torrent of images occurring within the frames of film suggests preconceived movie scenarios but proceeds without coherence. The lack of coherence, finally, is the quality that grips and stays with the reader; it is an assault on that flimsy linearity that is the currency of Hollywood, which makes of its illusions not art but lies.

"Lap Dissolves"
The final short subject, "Lap Dissolves," is longer still. It is an amusing series of ten overlapping dissolves, beginning with a literal cliff-hanger and running almost seamlessly through a number of genre samplers: a good-natured gangster film, a psychopathic murder sequence, a pirate scene, a

bored country girl, science fiction, a lengthy account of a string of transformations in a dream experienced by the daughter of one of the characters, a western clip, and a bus ride in which the driver promises that they will be there soon—"*There?*"

The piece ends with that question. "Lap Dissolves" is another assault on movie linearity; the series of dissolves begins from nowhere and continues in the same direction, treating us along the way to a skewed scenery of filmic clichés that will never be quite the same for us again.

Charlie in the House of Rue

The next feature is billed as comedy, though existential horror peers through the cracks. *Charlie in the House of Rue*, like the preceding pieces, moves on a stream of transforming images in a world where nothing is fixed; and a dreamlike mobility prevails.[5] The Charlie Chaplin we know from silent films, though never directly named, finds himself in an opulent house. He wanders from room to room, helping himself to available goodies, cigars, drinks, but the people he encounters are all rueful, dour, closed off, indifferent to his polite approaches.

There is a fat, mustachioed cook glowering over a bowl of soup in the kitchen; an old, top-hatted, goateed man at the drink trolley in the library; a silent-flicks policeman wearing a helmet; an elegant lady (perhaps the ingenue of the book's opening piece); and a maid. Charlie's attempts at communication with these gloomy, unresponsive people begin to go awry; as he tries to repair the damage caused by his errors, things only get worse, in classic slapstick manner.

But matters escalate, and the situation becomes increasingly uncertain and bizarre. He reaches for one thing only to find it has been transformed, in a moment's lights-out darkness, to something else. He throws a pie in the face of the cook and discovers it is really the face of the elegant woman. Classic slapstick comedy situations abound, but with a twist of *huis-clos* surreality: bypassing Chaplin's sentimental underpinnings, the piece evokes true existential terror in a world of timeless repetitions and unpredictable transmutations.

Charlie has set the house in motion, a series of motions that he struggles vainly to keep up with. He discovers the elegant woman with a noose around her neck about to plunge off the balustrade. Desperately, he entertains her with a comic juggling act to distract her from her intentions. Her face softens, she watches, but he slips and accidentally knocks her over the balustrade, from which she twitches and writhes at the end of the rope.

He races about trying to cut her down, to save her, but is foiled in slap-stick fashion again and again. Events in the other rooms where he seeks help or tools to cut the rope become increasingly grotesque. The maid, naked now, attacks him with a pair of scissors and, trying to cut off his moustache, stabs his nostril. The policeman clubs him and himself with his billy club. The cook goes berserk, beating Charlie brutally with the corpse of a decapitated hare.

The lights go on and off from time to time, leaving an altered situation. Bloody and bruised, Charlie finds himself in the library, which is now in good order again despite his most recent unleashing of chaos there. But a coffin is in the center of the room. The lid slowly rises, and blackness shines from within. The corpse in it, the old goateed man from the drink trolley, begins to sit up, but the lid slips and decapitates him. The lid rises again, and the headless corpse climbs out (yet another of the book's resurrections).

Charlie flees and finds the elegant lady again, still hanging from the rope, dead now. He piles a chair on a table on a stand and shinnies up to cut her free, but the furniture topples out from beneath him. He grabs for the corpse and clings to it to keep from falling. He dangles there, bruised and bleeding, his pants down around his ankles, as the light fades and everything else with it. His weeping face seems to ask, "What kind of place is this? Who took the lights away? And why is everybody laughing?" (*ANM*, 111). If comedy is a mask for suffering, the two merge here and are both illuminated. Charlie's wanting to know why everybody is laughing, while he clings to a hanged corpse, brings to mind Eliot's "laceration / Of laughter at what ceases to amuse."[6]

Charlie in the House of Rue is a remarkable accomplishment. Perhaps more than any other piece in the book, it reproduces the experience of film at the same time that it clearly transcends the natural and imposed limitations of that medium. The story reaches deep into the heart of the material for an experience far more profoundly moving than Chaplin was able or willing to try and, in doing so, turns popular culture into an astonishing piece of innovative art.

"Intermission"

The reader is advised of a moment's pause while the operator changes reels. While the reader-viewer waits, Coover presents "Intermission."

The piece begins, appropriately enough, with a young woman at the movies going to the lobby during intermission for refreshments. There she meets a man who invites her outside, where she is kidnapped by gangsters. Nearly 20 pages follow of preposterous events experienced by this character reminiscent of Terry Southern's *Candy* (1955), let loose in Spielberg's *Raiders of the Lost Ark* (1981): naive scenes of jungle dramas, escapes, Valentino abductions, more escapes, romances, near drownings, a further escape in a hot-air balloon from which she falls out over the movie house, half naked, nearly starved, just in time for the end of the intermission.

But something strange has happened. A cartoon is showing, but no one is laughing (the opposite of the situation that concludes *Charlie in the House of Rue*). The theater is full of dead people with flattened faces. She is about to scream when she feels a clawlike grip on her shoulder (Cope's link-and-claw theory again [147–48], though wearing thin).

At first she is frightened, but finally she realizes that "the claw only wants her to watch the movie, and hey, she's been watching movies all her life, so why stop now, right? Besides, isn't there always a happy ending? Has to be. It comes with the price of the ticket" (*ANM*, 134).

The amusement here seems as light as what it parodies, and it moves us breezily to the following piece.

"Cartoon"

"Cartoon,"—the same film perhaps that the heroine of "Intermission" sits watching in the icy clutches of the claw, waiting for her happy ending—begins: "The cartoon man drives his cartoon car into the cartoon town and runs over a real man" (*ANM*, 135). Coover once again brings to mind another recent Spielberg epic, *Who Killed Roger Rabbit?* (1988), in which a real actor drives into an eerily convincing "Toon Town." Spielberg dazzles with technical wizardry, but Coover is doing deeper work with the concepts of reality, realism, and fiction.

The cartoon man in a cartoon car in a cartoon town runs over a real man. Wronged, but not badly hurt (he compares it to a paper cut), the real man fetches a cartoon policeman while the cartoon man gets a real cop. A huge cartoon dog chases off the cartoon policeman while the real policeman proceeds to arrest the real man. A real cat chases the cartoon dog, but is in turn chased by a cartoon woman who seduces the real policeman by removing and giving him her cartoon breasts, which he has ogled with cartoon eyes after shooting the real cat.

The cartoon woman goes off with the cartoon dog as the cartoon man sets a cartoon dinner table for the real man, getting him to place the dead cat on it; when he does so, the cutlery runs off screaming. The real man leaves in the cartoon car, which has shrunk to handsize by the time he gets home. He finds his wife in bed with a cartoon man, which experience, she indicates, hurts as little as being hit by a cartoon car (like a paper cut).

"Ah," says the real man, and he "feels a stinging somewhere, though perhaps only in his reflections" (*ANM*, 138). He hears a policeman's whistle, "but he knows this is no solution, real or otherwise. It would be like scratching an itch with legislation or an analogy" (*ANM*, 139). In the mirror, he sees he has grown a pair of cartoon ears "like butterfly wings," which he wags "animatedly ... or perhaps being wiggled by them," thinking there is hope for him yet (*ANM*, 139).

The illusion here is achieved by the juxtaposition of the words *real* and *cartoon*. The reader responds to the cue words automatically, envisioning a "real" man in interchange with an "unreal" one (a cartoon figure), but in fact our real man is nothing but the noun, *man*. This "man" performs the acts of verbs; for example, he walks alongside the cartoon policeman, concerned about the cartoon policeman being suspended above the pavement. The reader "sees" a real man walking sensibly beside an impossible comic figure, but in fact the two figures, a cartoon and a noun, are equally comic. The straightman is even skimpier than the comic. One thinks of Gass's remark that discovering that characters in fiction are only words is something like suddenly discovering that one's wife is made of rubber (27).

The question seems to be how are we "real" persons affected by our interchanges with "cartoon" (or fictional) characters? Perhaps we begin to grow cartoon ears (with which to listen to reality) or find that our "reflections" (mimesis) "sting." If half the world around us has grown flat as a cartoon in our eyes, and if what we see in the "mirror" finally is turning into a fiction, where do we turn to find what is "real," to find something that can affect us more profoundly than a paper cut?

It is interesting to reflect that this might well have been the cartoon that "the claw" forced the heroine of "Intermission" to watch. That young woman, whose experience is as unreal as a movie romance or a weekly serial, sits in a movie palace full of corpses, confident that if she only continues to watch the film the happy ending she has paid for with her ticket will come along.

"Milford Junction, 1939: A Brief Encounter"

From the cartoon we turn to what the movies used to give us as "realism"—the travelogue. "Milford Junction, 1939: A Brief Encounter," however, is a travelogue superimposed upon the dim background of Noel Coward's *Brief Encounter* (1944). The result is a parody so dry it is barely humorous, combined with a drama so vague it is barely discernible.

As often as not, either the subjects of the old trailer travelogues, like Milford Junction (or Churley or Ketchworth, the other towns mentioned in the narration) were hardly worthy of such attention, or the filmic rendering was so inept as to render the place a drab and unlikely tourist site.

Coover plays with the inanity of the narrator's monologue in such films, cleverly achieving glimpses beneath the dim surface. The parody, however, seems to suffer from a degree of the oppressive, pointless, forced dramatic detail of its object. Readers interested in an appreciation of the piece are referred to Cope (145–47), who seems to find some greater virtue in it.

"Top Hat"

In "Top Hat" dance becomes fiction and movement metaphor, though again, as always, the dance here is in language, in words.[7] This is one of the dazzlements of this book: Coover's skill at transforming film genre into fiction. There is a sharp irony in his bringing this off in a culture where film is the ultimate medium, where the highest praise of a fiction is its selection for adaptation to film, the more expensive the better, dismal as such adaptations generally are.

But Coover successfully adapts in the opposite direction, bringing Fred Astaire from silver screen to book page and pitting him, as a maverick in white tails, against the establishment, achieving what the loner in contemporary American myth is no longer allowed: victory over the crowd.

"You Must Remember This"

Our *Night at the Movies* concludes with "You Must Remember This," a fictional reworking of what is probably the most prominent film myth of the post-World War II era, *Casablanca*.

A number of insinuated elements in the film become explicit in the fiction, and the result is general destruction of the story and disorientation of the characters. Ilsa Lund appears to Rick as in the film, requests the letters of transit as in the film, pleads, demands, and threatens as in the film, and, as in the film, Rick defies the pistol in her hand and overpowers her with the sheer moral force of his stance. But then things begin to go awry when Rick breaks the code of romance: he takes hold of Ilsa's breasts and thrusts his pelvis into her buttocks.

"Is this right?" she gasps. "I—I don't know!" he groans. "I can't think!" (*ANM*, 161).

The story turns from romantic implication to sexual explicitness. There follow some 20 pages of sexual abandon; scenes of Ilsa and Rick partaking of one another in most conceivable manners are intellectualized as a Norman Mailer might have done in homage to a Henry Miller.

After an act of ultimate passion on the floor of Rick's apartment ("It was the best fokk I effer haf," says Ilsa [*ANM*, 164]), Ilsa muses that the fine carpet is stained. "What of it?" says Rick nonchalantly (166). Ilsa mounts the bidet and soaps and splashes herself while Rick stands sans-culottes in his white dinner jacket, letters of transit in the breast pocket, sipping a straight whiskey. Rick sees her haunches "like archways to heaven or an image of eternity" (*ANM*, 172), as well as visions on the screen of her fresh-washed buttocks. His "link-and-claw theory" (again!) of time is developed: "not a ceaseless flow but a rapid series of electrical leaps across tiny gaps between discontinuous bits" (*ANM*, 173).

The romantic theory is hilariously undone, and the legend deromanticized with brilliant comic meditations (despite the tin Norwegian accent given Ilsa—nearly as dismal as Meryl Streep's Karen Blixen). Rick and Ilsa are left in a kind of contemporary manual of good bedroom manners in the age of erotic enlightenment before the era of HIV.

Slowly, however, the force of their passion, as passion's force will, begins to dwindle. The background music ("As Time Goes By") begins to have the annoying effect of "mice in the wall" (*ANM*, 180), last heard from in "After Lazarus." Ilsa begins to wonder how she got mixed up with Rick in the first place; perhaps it was simply because "he seemed so happy when she took hold of his penis" in Paris (*ANM*, 183). She speculates on why he takes things so seriously and expects to understand things, as Americans do. "He is an innocent man, after all. This is probably his first affair" (*ANM*, 184). Rick, too, begins to have his doubts. "Maybe she was stupider than he thought" (*ANM*, 185).

Finally, they discover that the story has gone wrong. All of the other characters, those from Casablanca as well as those from Paris, are waiting expectantly downstairs in the bar for Rick and Ilsa to play their part. Ilsa's identity begins to dissolve as she becomes conscious of the fiction she is participating in. "Maybe," Rick muses, "making up stories is a way to keep . . . from going insane" (*ANM*, 180). "Maybe memory itself is a kind of trick, something that turns illusion into reality and makes the real world vanish before everyone's eyes like magic" (*ANM*, 179).

In the end, they realize that the story, the memories, have gone awry, and they try to resume the lines of the script that has given them their legendary identity. But their cover is blown; their identities and their world have vanished "like magic."

"You Must Remember This" is a strong comic close to the collection. It is a fictional examination of a Hollywood legend that perhaps more than any other has taken hold of the imagination of the postwar Western world, convincing us that we believe the individual memory of pleasure and happiness is less important than our responsibility to serve and preserve the democratic society in which we live.

But, Coover seems to say, the roles assigned us by that legend do not quite fit. Self-denigration is not a mask we easily don in reality. In recent years society has been ruled by pleasure and memory has become a trick, supported by Hollywood, to turn illusion into reality so convincingly that we no longer quite know what the nature of the real world is: It has disappeared as if by magic.

"And then?" (*ANM*, 187).

This sums up well the task Coover has taken upon himself in his volumes of short fiction. By disrupting the traditional flow of the legends that define us, he challenges the reader to define him- or herself. He takes our "mythic residue" away from us and leaves us with a question—the question on the lips of every listener squatting around the fire listening to every storyteller: "And then?"

That is Coover's answer for us. The very question.

Coover's major collections of short fiction span nearly 20 years from the first volume to the third, and their concerns throughout are metafictional. They deal, via illusion, with the techniques and illusions of popular fiction and film that we use to create our identities. Coover plays with these popular illusions to attract the reader into a fiction where those established, conventional ploys will be stripped away, bringing the reader into confrontation with deeper functioning levels of fiction. In the end perhaps little more remains after the old illusions have been stripped away than new illusions.

Nonetheless, the process frees us of that Coleridgian film of familiarity that dulls the force of conventional fiction. We are delivered to the strange new existential magic that awaits us in Coover's elevators, behind his pulsing doors, in his reworked fables, fairy tales, and biblical humanizations, in his verbal renderings of TV game shows, cartoons, silent movies, and Hollywood films, and amidst the ruins of his fictional islands, where destruction becomes an act of creation, the only possible beginning an end.

It is difficult to imagine American short fiction over the past three decades without Robert Coover. He emerged with the wave of innovation of the 1960s, but his work is not like that of the other innovators of that time. In fact, his work is not quite like anything seen before, though his influence continues to prevail. In his tales, which frighten us and make us laugh and never quite satisfy, we find an antidote for the mental poison of our times.

Notes to Part 1

Introduction

1. Robert Coover, *Pricksongs & Descants* (New York: E. P. Dutton, 1969), abbreviated here as *P&D*, with page references to the 1970 New American Library Plume edition.

2. Cf. Thomas Kennedy, "Interview, 1989," in part 2 of this book.

3. *Norman Mailer, The Armies of the Night: History as a Novel, the Novel as History* (New York: New American Library, 1968).

4. William H. Gass, *Fiction and the Figures of Life* (New York: Knopf, 1970), 27, hereafter cited in the text, with page references to the 1972 Vintage edition.

5. Bill Bufford, editorial in *Dirty Realism, New Writing from America: Granta* 8 (1983): 4–5, hereafter cited in text.

6. David Applefield, interview with Raymond Carver, *Frank: An International Journal of Contemporary Writing and Art* 8/9 (Winter 1987–88): 9.

7. Curtis White and Ron Sukenik, "Is Realism 'State Fiction?'" *Colorado Review* NSXV:2 (Fall–Winter 1988): 1–12.

8. Donald Barthelme, "Not Knowing," in The Pushcart Prize XI (Wainscot, N.Y., 1986), 25–27.

9. Bruno Bettelheim, *The Uses of Enchantment* (New York: Penguin, 1968), 61, hereafter cited in the text.

10. Lawrence Millman, cited from an unpublished interview with the author, 1985.

11. Robert Coover, *A Night at the Movies or, You Must Remember This* (New York: Simon & Schuster, 1987), abbreviated here as *ANM*, with page references to the 1988 Collier Books edition.

Pricksongs & Descants

1. Neil Schmitz, "Robert Coover and the Hazards of Metafiction," *Novel* 7 (Spring 1974): 214.

2. Jackson I. Cope, Robert Coover's Fiction (Baltimore: Johns Hopkins University Press, 1986), 11.

3. For the purposes of this discussion I have numbered the scenes. I refer to those numbers as well as the page numbers to help give a sense of sequential "place" to the scene under discussion. I believe this facilitates a discussion of this fiction, whose narrative structure is dense and nonlinear.

4. Richard Andersen, *Robert Coover* (Boston: Twayne Publishers, 1981), 99, hereafter cited in the text.

5. William H. Gass, "The Concept of Character in Fiction," in Gass, *Fiction and Figures*, 45.

6. E. M. Forster, *Aspects of the Novel* (New York: (Harcourt, Brace & World, 1927), 94; Herbert Gold, "Vladimir Nabokov: An Interview," The Art of Fiction XL, *Paris Review* 41 (Summer–Fall 1967): 96.

7. Wallace Stevens, "Peter Quince at the Clavier," in *The American Tradition in Literature*, vol. 2 (New York: W. W. Norton, 1967), 1529.

8. Lois Gordon, *Robert Coover: The Universal Fictionmaking Process* (Carbondale: South Illinois University Press, 1983), 99.

9. A. E. Houseman, "Terence, This Is Stupid Stuff," in *A Shropshire Lad* (London, 1896).

10. James Joyce, *Ulysses* [1922] (New York: Modern Library, 1934).

11. Ibid.

12. Cf. "Prologue," "Seven Exemplary Fictions" (*P&D*, 77).

13. Thomas E. Kennedy, "Interview, 1989," in part 2 of this book.

14. Frank Gado, *First Person: Conversations on Writers and Writing* (New York: Union College Press, 1973), 146–47.

15. Marianne Moore, "Poetry" (original version), in *The Complete Poems* (new York: Macmillan/Viking, 1967), 266–67.

16. Eliphas Levy, *The Doctrine and Ritual of Magic*, quoted in Richard Cavendish, *The Black Arts* (New York: Pedigree, 1967), 31.

17. When the 22-year-old Joyce left Ireland in 1904, he said, "I will not serve that in which I no longer believe, whether it calls itself my home, my fatherland, or my church; and I will try to express myself in some mode of life or art as freely as I can and as wholly as I can, using for my dissent the only arms I allow myself to use—silence, exile, and cunning." Quoted in *The European*, 11–13 January 1991, 7.

18. R. H. W. Dillard, "Robert Coover," *Hollins Critic* 7, no. 2 (April 1970): 3, hereafter cited in the text.

19. Gordon Weaver, "The Parts of Speech," in *A World Quite Round* (Baton Rouge: Louisiana State University Press, 1986), 92.

In Bed One Night & Other Brief Encounters

1. Robert Coover, *In Bed One Night & Other Brief Encounters* (Providence, R.I.: Burning Deck Press, 1983), abbreviated here as *IBON*.

2. First published in *Panache* (1971).

3. First published in *Panache* (1973).

4. First published in *Playboy* (1980).

5. First published in *Antaeus* (1977).

6. First published in *Triquarterly* 35 (Winter 1976): 79.

7. First published in *Panache* (1971).

8. First published in *Panache* (1977).

9. Robert Coover, 26 December 1989, personal correspondence with the author.

10. First published in *Harper's* 244 (March 1972): 82–87.

A Night at the Movies

1. Except where otherwise specified, the stories in this collection appeared originally in periodical form in *Evergreen Review, Triquarterly, Paris Exiles, Frank,* and *Playboy.*

2. First published in chapbook form (Bruccoli-Clark, 1980).

3. First published, as "The Mex Would Arrive at Gentry's at 12:10," in *Evergreen Review* 47 (June 1967): 63–65, 98–102.

4. C. G. Jung, *Memories, Dreams, Reflections* (London: Flamingo Books, 1983), 52–56.

5. First published in chapbook form (Lincoln, Mass., Penmaen Press, 1980).

6. T. S. Eliot, "Little Gidding," *Four Quartets,* 2:83–84.

7. First published in *Frank: An International Journal of Contemporary Writing and Art* 6–7 (Winter–Spring 1987): 12–16.

Part 2

THE WRITER

Introduction

The three interviews that follow here span the decade from the end of the 1970s to the end of the 1980s.

The first and longest, Larry McCaffery's 1979 exchange of views with Coover, probes deeply into the writer's ideas about metafiction and his concern not so much with language per se as with fiction's reflection of "gesture, connections, paradox, story." It also deals with a number of matters not otherwise touched upon in this book, including Coover's views on playwriting and screenwriting and some of his experiences in the writing and publication of his great novel, *The Public Burning*. I believe that Coover's description of these experiences is relevant to an understanding not only of his fiction but of the situation of all writers who are thought to "violate" certain narrow conventions of theme and technique. Considering the recent attacks on artistic freedom made by people like Jesse Helms through the National Endowment for the Arts and the attempt to limit freedom of expression to the political, it is particularly interesting to hear of the prepublication reaction to Coover's "political" writing.

The second interview, conducted by David Applefield in 1986, deals primarily with socioliterary issues such as the American college-writing phenomenon and the (then) new conservatism in America. The interview also includes a rundown of Coover's estimation of other American writers.

The prime aim of the third and shortest interview, my own, conducted in 1989, was to explore a couple of specific technical questions about the writing of fiction and about the writer's own perception of the process.

I hope and believe that the three interviews combine to give a fair overview of Coover as a fiction writer and of his sense of himself and his work in relationship to contemporary American society and literary history. I would once again like to express my appreciation to Larry McCaffery and David Applefield for generously permitting me to reprint these portions of their fine interviews.

Interview, 1979

Larry McCaffery

... Robert Coover is one of the most intense literary figures anyone is likely to encounter. After an evening of drinking wine and exchanging anecdotes at his house with his close friends Robert Scholes, Jack Hawkes, and their wives, we met for our interview at the ancient lounge of the Brown University English department. Bob led the way through the labyrinthine corridors of this building to his office, with its unobtrusive, unmarked door. Coover is a rather short, slightly built man with thick brown hair and a quick, boyish smile that makes him look fifteen years younger than his forty-eight years. In answering questions, he spoke with passionate and confident conviction; although he chose his words carefully, Coover expressed his opinions forcefully. All around us—on his desk, the walls, even the floor—were note cards and manuscript pages, written in different colored inks, from his various works in progress. ...

LM: You've done most of your writing during the past ten or fifteen years while living in England and Spain. Are there any advantages to being an expatriate writer?

RC: Detachment mainly. A writer needs isolation, a cell of his own, that's obvious, but distance can also help. It has a way of freeing the imagination, stirring memory. Fewer localisms creep in, less passing trivia, transient concerns. Personally, I don't seem to be able to cut myself off very well here in the States. I get too engaged in things around me and end up having less time to write, less energy for it. It can work both ways, of course. If you're not careful you can stay away too long and lose touch. No easy answer.

LM: You say in your "Introduction" to the Fiction Collective's *Statements Two* that "in America, art, like everything else (knowledge, condoms, religions, etc.) is a product. The discovery of this is the capstone to the artist's

An interview with Robert Coover, by Larry McCaffery, in *Anything Can Happen: Interviews with Contemporary American Novelists,* conducted and edited by Tom LeClair and Larry McCaffery, Urbana, Chicago, London: University of Illinois Press, ©1983 by the Board of Trustees of the University of Illinois.

alienation process in America." I take it from this that you feel that the commodity mentality of American culture makes it even more difficult to be an artist here than elsewhere—in Europe, for example.

RC: Yes—in fact, many Europeans have been shocked at their own transformations when they enter the American market. Of course, art's treated as a commodity throughout most of the Western world—and elsewhere, maybe even worse—but in America the market's so vast and impersonal. To most Americans the publishing industry is as strange and remote as Oz, but it's also true the other way around: to the industry, the American public is like a magical and unpredictable fairyland, "out there somewhere," complete with a fabulous buried treasure just waiting to be dug up. There is no common language or concern between them; their only exchange is barter. A writer exists as a kind of icon, or else as nothing. If this, or something like it, happened to a writer in Europe, he would at least have his own intellectual community to fall back on. Here we have no such communities—nor is there any real hope for one. There's no place for it, no physical way to work it out. The nearest thing we have is the academic circuit, where the steady flow of jobs, readings, conferences, visiting lectureships, and so on, brings people together, but it's very loosely strung, and many people have no access to it. And besides, it's been drying up. We have no gathering places, no forum, no national magazines, no cafés, no boulevards. We do not get together and talk about things on national TV or radio. P.E.N. is trying to do something about it now, setting up local chapters, but the effort is necessarily full of artifice—a kind of thinking man's Rotary Club. We have no natural center.

LM: The Fiction Collective also seems to be trying to do what they can to change things. What do you think of their efforts to date?

RC: Well, it also has to compete in the marketplace. It doesn't have much time for anything else. And its people are scattered and they lack the money for getting everybody together. It should be a more exciting phenomenon than it is, but it's still largely a publishing maneuver. As such, though, important. Probably, overall, they've put out the best list in town.

LM: On the other hand, you've also said that you feel there's not much life in the fiction coming out of Europe today; yet American fiction, from my vantage point, has been enormously exciting during the '60s and '70s. Doesn't this seem contradictory to you?

RC: No. A writer may or may not be discouraged by isolation and alienation. If he goes on, he may even benefit from it. Highly communalized groups of intellectuals like you have in Europe probably put more pressure on their members to conform to certain standards, discouraging too much eccentricity or adventurism. The standards are probably higher, though, letting less shit through. It's like going to a very good school: you must learn what's being taught at that school, rather than striking out on your own. You gain discipline, knowledge, historical perspective, and so on, but you may lose a little confidence in your own imaginative potential. Besides, we may have been underestimating the quality of European fiction during this period when writing in the Americas seemed to be enjoying such a renaissance. After all, not only are there all the masters of the old forms, there are writers like Tournier and Beckett and Grass, Calvino, Carter, Gombrowicz, and so on. Perhaps we've also had an exaggerated notion of our own uniqueness and importance and quality. Novelty can hide a lot of flaws.

LM: But this renaissance you speak of—you've suggested that most of the important contemporary American writers weren't even aware of each other's works: so what was going on to generate this creative outburst?

RC: Well, many reasons probably. The postwar appetite for change and newness, the college boom and the money that was around—all those new English professors, for example, needing something to write about—and then little things like the Kafka phenomenon, Barney Rosset's Grove Press and the new paperback industry, the resurgence of interest in the surrealists, ease of travel, the explosion of all the new media, video especially. And then there was the general feeling, especially during the Cold War, of being stifled by dogma, the sense that so much of the trouble we found ourselves in was the consequence of not being imaginative enough about the ways out. Plus the threat of nuclear apocalypse: how could we go on thinking in the old trite ways when every day we had to imagine the unimaginable? All the disciplines were affected, not just writing. Physics, for example, had long since been leading the way . . .

LM: You mentioned the media. Obviously your fiction has been influenced by television, cinema, and theater. Were you consciously aiming at integrating elements from these other media?

RC: I think in part it was unconscious. Stories tend to appear to me, not as formal ideas, but as metaphors, and these metaphors seem to demand structures of their own: they seem to have an internal need for a certain form. Nevertheless, we've all been affected by film technology, the information bombardment of television, and so on, and certainly I've had a conscious desire to explore the ways all this makes our minds work.

LM: Can you say something more about these metaphors that your fiction grows out of?

RC: They're the germ, the thought, the image, the idea, out of which all the rest grows. They're always a bit elusive, involving thoughts, feelings, abstractions, visual material, all at once. I suppose they're a little like dream fragments, in that such fragments always contain, if you analyze them, so much more than at first you suspect. But they're not literally that—I never write from dreams. All these ideas come to me in the full light of day. Some, when you pry them open, have too little inside to work with. Others are unexpectedly fat and rich. Novels typically begin for me as very tiny stories or little one-act play ideas which I think at the time aren't going to fill three pages. Then slowly the hidden complexities reveal themselves.

. . . .

LM: One of your main thematic intentions seems to be to expose the so-called objective reports of history, news reporting, theological dictums, and so forth. You suggest that such reports result largely from man's desire to shape random events into some kind of pleasing pattern or design. Do you mean to suggest that all these spring from a central artistic impulse?

RC: I wouldn't say "artistic." Art's not nature after all. But, yes, the human need for pattern, and language's propensity, willy-nilly, for supplying it—what happens, I think, is that every effort to form a view of the world, every effort to speak of the world, involves a kind of fiction-making process. Memory is a kind of narrative, as is our perception of what the future is apt to bring us, our understanding of anything going on out in the world—even our scientific understanding of the world has to be reduced to a narrative of sorts in order to grasp it. What's a formula but a kind of sentence, a story among other possible stories? Men live by fictions. They have to. Life's too complicated, we just can't handle all the input, we have to isolate little bits and make reasonable stories out of them. Of course, that's an artificial act and therefore, you might say, "artistic." But I would say the impulse was from necessity, and only some of the resulting stories are "artistic." All of them, though, are merely artifices—that is, they are always in some ways false, or at best incomplete. There are always other plots, other settings, other interpretations. So if some stories start throwing their weight around, I like to undermine their authority a bit, work variations, call attention to their fictional natures.

LM: Is this your explanation for why we have had this outburst of self-reflexive fictions during the '60s and '70s?

RC: Yes. If storytelling is central to the human experience, stories about storytelling, or stories which talk about themselves as stories, become central, too. For a while anyway. I think, as a fashion, it's passing, though more self-reflexive fictions will be written.

LM: One of the frequent criticisms leveled against metafiction is that by concentrating on the act of writing, by becoming more involuted and self-conscious, it becomes narcissistic and evades the kinds of "moral issues" that John Gardner has recently championed. Do you feel that there is an inherent opposition between didactic and aesthetic aims in a work of fiction?

RC: No, it's a phony issue. John's a moral fiction-writer—some of the time; probably not often enough—but he's an immoral moralist. He knows this debate about "entertainment" and "instruction" is a terribly old, seedy issue, a kind of political game at its worst, that goes back to the ancients. Who's to say, for example, that self-reflexive fiction, dealing as it assumes it does with a basic human activity, is not, by examining that activity as it celebrates it, engaged in a very moral act?

LM: But you wouldn't insist that good fiction must be moral in the way that Gardner suggests it must—that is, by creating heroic models, proposing solutions to issues rather than simply raising them, or whatever?

RC: I would not, myself, say that fiction *must* anything. Ever.

LM: I find your fiction repeatedly returning to a central situation. We observe a character or characters engaged in this subjective, fiction-making process we have just been talking about. In their desire for stability and order, however, they lose sight of what they have been doing and begin to insert these fictions into the world as dogma; this winds up entrapping or even destroying them. Is this a fair reading?

RC: Yes. Why not?

LM: Why do you return so often to this idea?

102

RC: To the scene of the crime, you mean? A weakness, no doubt, a lack of moral fiber. Maybe the struggle I had as a young writer against the old forms made me overly aware of their restrictive nature, such that I found myself burdened with a vast number of metaphoric possibilities, all of which were touched by this sense of dogma invading the world and turning it to stone. But I have literally hundreds of ideas, virtually every day I think of another one, so maybe I'll get lucky next time, choose one with a different bloom. It's the choice that scares me. I mean, we only have so many lives to lead. *The [Origin of the] Brunists* took me four years, *The Public Burning* longer. If I could work through all the ideas I have now without thinking up any more (and as I said that, damn it, I've just thought of another one), I'd need a couple of hundred years more at least. Like human seed: a billion kids eager to be born every minute, but you only get a few at best.

LM: The first things you ever published were a series of poems in *The Fiddlehead*. Since then you've worked with drama, movie scripts, translation, and various other literary forms. Which ones have you found the most interesting to work with, and what are the most important differences among them?

RC: The central thing for me is story. I like poems, paintings, music, even buildings, that tell stories. I believe, to be good, you have to master the materials of the form you're working in, whether it's language, form and color, meter, stone, cameras, lights, or inks, but all that's secondary to me. Necessary but secondary. I know there's a way of looking at fiction as being made up of words, and that therefore what you do with words becomes the central concern. But I'm much more interested in the way that fiction, for all its weaknesses, reflects something else—gesture, connections, paradox, story. I work with language because paper is cheaper than film stock. And because it's easier to work with a committee of one. But storytelling doesn't have to be done with words on a printed page, or even with spoken words: we all learned that as kids at our Saturday morning religious experience in the local ten-cent cinemas. Probably, if I had absolute freedom to do what I want, I'd prefer film.

LM: What is it that excites you so much about film?

RC: First of all, its great immediacy: it grasps so much with such rapidity. Certainly it's the medium par excellence for the mimetic narrative. And it has a relationship with time that is fascinating—we can take in centuries in an hour or two, even in a few minutes. All narratives play with time, but only film can truly juggle it. So: a mix of magic and documentary power. And I don't dislike the communal aspect of film, the bringing together of a lot of different talents to produce a work of art—it's healthier somehow than that deep-closeted ego involvement of the novelist, poet, or painter. But the problem, of course, is that it's so expensive and potentially so profitable. Too many non-creative types get in on the processes; more than one good film's been ruined by them. The tales of woe from writers misused by the film industry are beyond number.

LM: What about your experiences with the theater?

RC: Like film, it's terribly destructive of creative time. You find yourself working long hours over five or six lines that took you maybe fifteen minutes to write. And before that there's the casting, the designing of the set, struggles with producers and directors, costumes, music maybe—and if you're going to get seriously involved with theater, you've got to get involved with all of it. But there's something exhilarating about it, too—it's a kind of Pygmalion experience, seeing it come alive before your eyes. And all the performing arts have the excitement of ephemerality. Novelists sometimes get this sense of the weightiness of their task, as though they were chipping their work out of stone—one slip and it's all ruined forever. Contrarily, every night at the theater it's all brand new—and when it's over, it's gone, except as it exists in the memory, so long as that lasts. It gives me a sense of living in the present that I rarely get as a novelist.

LM: Have you ever gotten involved in the productions of your plays?

RC: Yes, several times, most intensely a few years ago in the New York production of *The Kid* at the American Place Theatre. Jack Gelber was the director, and working with him and with Wynn Handman, who ran the theater, was one of the happiest experiences in my life. We made a mistake in the casting which proved to be troublesome, and there were a few decisions made that maybe weren't wise ones, but there's always going to be this—if we did it again, there would be others, that's part of the fun of it. For the most part, it was a wonderful show, greatly enhanced by all the talents that contributed to it. Jack got an Obie for directing it and the production won several other awards. It was a real treat. I was also very modestly involved in a wonderful production of *Love Scene* in Paris, where it premiered, there called *Scene d'amour*. It was directed by Henri Gilabert in a little Left Bank theater called the Troglodyte and with such intelligence and balance that it was like seeing before my eyes—and in French at that—exactly what I'd envisioned in my mind before. *Rip Awake* premiered out in Los Angeles where Ron Sossi played Rip, and his Odyssey group also premiered *A Theological Position.*

LM: I'm sure you heard of the scandal that surrounded *A Theological Position*'s production out there.

RC: Yes, well, Ron probably asked for it by including it in what he called "An Evening of Dirty Religious Plays," but my work's had a long history of suppression or bowdlerization, so I'm used to it. Actually, I don't see it as a scandalous play—there's nothing new about talking cunts, after all. Probably, for some of the people on the council out there, the image struck too close to home. Anyway, it's a good theater group, and I hope to work more with them.

LM: Those Western materials you used in *The Kid* you've also used in other stories, and you return repeatedly to fairy tales, sports, and other elements that are usually seen as pop-cultural material. What's the source of your fascination with this kind of stuff?

RC: It's all material that's close to the mythic content of our lives, and is therefore an important part of our day-to-day fiction-making process. The pop culture we absorb in childhood—and I'd include all the pop religions as well—goes on affecting the way we respond to the world or talk about it for the rest of our lives. And this mythology of ours, this unwritten Bible, is being constantly reinforced by books and newspapers, films, television, advertisements, politicians, teachers, and so on. So working inside these forms is a way of staying close to the bone.

LM: What about your interest in another concept that recurs in your fiction—the concept of number and its inevitable companion, numerology? These both seem to be perfect examples of what you described earlier as fictions man uses to navigate through the world.

RC: Yes, or to stumble through it. It's one way among many that the mind gets locked into fixed distorting patterns. Silly stuff. But it was an important element in the Christian apocalyptic vision, so it had to be part of the *Brunists*. Then, once I started working with it, I found it again in a lot of secondary and ironic ways. Especially in the formal design.

LM: You mean like Calvino's use of tarot images in *The Castle of Crossed Destinies?* He seems to be using tarot in that book as a generating formal design in much the same way that you use number theory in a story like "The Elevator."

RC: Mmm. Tarot exists in the *Brunists,* too. You remember the widows of the miners gathered at Mabel's and sat around her cards in the key chapter of the section called "The Sign." It's also in the structure. Number presents itself more directly; you recognize it more quickly.

LM: What about your apparent interest in puns and wordplay? Freud maintains that one derives pleasure from the pun or the play on words by following the possibilities and transformations implicit in language. Gombrich describes this process as "the juxtaposition of concepts which one arrives at casually, unexpectedly, unleashes a preconscious idea." Does your fascination with puns have to do with this view of the transformational possibilities lying within the formal properties of languages?

RC: I was more fascinated just now with the Gombrich quote. It's a painterly thought: the shock of strange juxtapositions. I like the pun for its intense condensation, but for me it's only a second-rate version of the more exciting idea of the juxtaposition of two unexpected elements—structural puns, you might call them. A lot of my stories begin this way. Again the use of seeming paradox, the vibrant space between the poles.

LM: Is that how "The Panel Game" got started? It's obviously very much concerned with this business of wordplay.

RC: Yes, but it's an early breakaway story for me, so it's more self-conscious than most. I was struggling to do something I had never done before, and it shows. All seven of the stories in that little "Exemplary Fictions" section of Pricksongs are discovery stories like that, blind launchings-forth, as it were. I only selected those that seemed unique turning-points. "The Panel Game" is a mid-1950s story, and the next one in that group is already from the 1960s, with a lot missing in between.

LM: You wrote me once that "The Panel Game" was an important early story for you, and when I looked back at it, it seemed to contain the seeds of a lot of the central motifs in your later work—the struggle with transformation, the attempt to unravel a structure encoded in symbols, the game metaphor, and so on.

RC: Yes, well, Borges said we go on writing the same story all our lives. The trouble is, it's usually a story that can never be told—there's always this distance between the sign and the signified, it's the oldest truth in philosophy—and that's why we tend to get so obsessive about it. The important thing is to accept this unbridgeable distance and carry on with the crazy bridge-building just the same.

. . . .

LM: Critics and reviewers have often remarked on this surprising empathy they feel for Nixon. How did you choose him to be your central narrator in *The Public Burning?*

RC: I'm not sure whether it was a matter of choice or necessity—he emerged from the texts, as it were. He has a way of doing that, fighting his way to the center stage; it's hard to stop him. Nevertheless, there were other possibilities. The book began as a little theater idea which grew into a series of rather raucous circus acts. I began to feel the need for a quieter voice to break in from time to time. I wanted someone who lived inside the mythology, accepting it, and close to the center, yet not quite in the center, off to the edge a bit, an observer. A number of characters auditioned for the part, but Nixon, when he appeared, proved ideal.

LM: Why was that?

RC: Well, for one thing he's such a self-conscious character. He has to analyze everything, work out all the parameters. He worries about things—and then there's his somewhat suspicious view of the world. He doesn't trust people very much—often for good reason. He lives in a world where trust is often misplaced, and he learned early to trust no one. And that included Eisenhower, J. Edgar Hoover, the whole government and judicial establishment. This attitude of his allowed me to reach skeptical conclusions through him about what was happening at the time of the Rosenberg executions, conclusions which would have been difficult from other viewpoints. For Eisenhower, if the FBI and the courts said so, then the Rosenbergs were guilty, they had to be. But Nixon could doubt this. He could imagine that his best ally, a man like Hoover, say, might not be letting him see everything. He could see the case in terms of who stood to gain what from it. And, of course, I also had it on faith from the beginning that any exploration of Nixon, this man who has played such a large role in American society since World War II, would have to reveal something about us all. It was another quality, though, that first called him forth in my mind—this was in 1969, just after he'd been elected president—and that was his peculiar talent for making a fool of himself.

LM: You've spoken of seeing him as a kind of clown . . .

RC: Yes. I was developing this series of circus acts—all these verbal acrobatics, death-defying highwire acts, showy parades, and so on—and I needed a clown to break in from time to time and do a few pratfalls. He was perfect for this. For a while, anyway. Eventually his real-life pratfalls nearly undid my own; I couldn't keep up with him. Had I been able to finish the book in time to publish it in 1972—as a kind of election-year gift to the incumbent, as it were—life would have been a lot easier. On the other hand, the Watergate episode forced me to work a lot harder, dig deeper, think beyond the pratfalls. So I probably ended up with a better book. Dearly as it cost me.

LM: Your novella, "Whatever Happened to Gloomy Gus of the Chicago Bears," appeared in the *American Review* during this period when you were working on *The Public Burning,* and it also deals with Nixon. Was it originally conceived as an integral part of your bigger project?

RC: No, it was completely separate, though there is a writerly connection in that I used it to work off some of my frustrations with *The Public Burning.* One of the peculiarities of *The Public Burning* was that it was made up of thousands and thousands of tiny fragments that had to be painstakingly stitched together, and it was not hard to lose patience with it. It was like a gigantic impossible puzzle. I was striving for a text that would seem to have been written by the whole nation through all its history, as though the sentences had been forming themselves all this time, accumulating toward this experience. I wanted thousands of echoes, all the sounds of the nation. Well, the idea was good, but the procedures were sometimes unbelievably tedious. And at some low point I got a request from a popular magazine for a sports story. (That's what happens when you write a book with "baseball" in the title.) I turned them down, of course, but the idea stuck in my head somewhere and niggled at me. One of the most successful failures in Nixon's life had been his abortive high school and college football career, but I hadn't found much space for it in *The Public Burning.* In an idle moment I married this to his belief that if you just work hard enough at something you could achieve it, and considered an alternate career for him as a pro football player. As this would had to have taken place in the 1930s, it suddenly opened up for me the possibility of writing a good old-fashioned 1930s-style novella, full of personal material, thoughtful asides, and so on. Everything fell into place like magic, and I sat down at the machine and for the first time in years just banged happily away. It was the most joyful writing experience I ever had. It was very refreshing and probably helped me get on through to the end of *The Public Burning.*

LM: There must have been some moments when you felt you'd never finish *The Public Burning* . . .

RC: Oh yes, many times. The worst moment was probably when Hal Scharlatt, my editor at Dutton, died. Hal was a man with a lot of strengths and he was very supportive. He was the only man, I felt, who would ever publish this book. And he was a friend. When he died suddenly, a young man still, I went through a very sorrowful time. It was as though all the props had been pulled out from under this monstrous thing I was building, and I was about to be flattened by it. I no longer believed it would be published, and I had to write against this certainty. And I was very nearly right.

LM: Your problems in getting the book published after you finished it are already nearly legendary. What happened, from your perspective?

RC: It's a complicated story, but at its heart is a betrayal by my editor at Knopf, Bob Gottlieb. He failed to stand by me or the book when it counted, and so cost me a lot of harassment and a couple of years of my writing life. The book was finished in 1975. That summer, with a lot of seeming enthusiasm, Gottlieb wrestled the manuscript away from Dutton, promising to publish it in 1976, during the Bicentennial and the presidential election. I was living in England at the time and made a trip back to the States at my own expense that autumn in order to complete the editing with Gottlieb and with Ted Solotaroff of Bantam, the company involved in the paperback rights. But then, with the book going into production just after Christmas, the RCA and Random House corporation lawyers began putting pressure on Knopf, and Gottlieb soon knuckled under, even suggesting to me on the phone that the book might after all be "immoral." I understand that the final decision to suppress the book came from the Random House boss Bob Bernstein, who shortly thereafter won a Freedom of the Press award. The book went from house to house then, amid a lot of false rumors, getting rejected by one set of corporation lawyers after another. I finally had to return to the States myself to sort it out. By then I'd already lost over a year, the Bicentennial which might have cushioned its publication had passed, and the book had become a kind of notorious hot potato. Eventually Richard Seaver convinced Viking to do the book. There were a lot of conditions. They refused to pay off Knopf, for example, on the reasonable grounds that Knopf had broken their contract with me and were owed nothing—indeed, they had even made it more difficult to get the book published successfully. Viking also held all my moneys due in escrow for several years in case of legal costs, for which they held me 100 percent responsible. At the same time, the house lawyers did everything they could to pressure me to emasculate the book, though in the end, thanks mainly to Dick Seaver with support from Tom Guizburg, the book did go through and was given a good production. As for Knopf, they still held Bantam to the old contract and refused to let them go—and thus, in effect, since Bantam's support was the key to Viking's willingness to do the book, refused to let the book be published at all—until I signed a separate statement saying that I owed them all advances paid. I am still paying off that debt today. Finally, two-and-a-half disruptive years after I had finished it, the book appeared.

LM: You just mentioned that the house lawyers tried to "emasculate" the book. Did they succeed in directly affecting your aesthetic decisions—say, in the final process?

RC: No. There were a lot of unpleasant pressures, but they were resisted. Dick Seaver was a big help in this, acting as a buffer against the worst of it. Both he and Solotaroff were very helpful editors, two of the few good editors left in the industry. The book needed cutting and we worked hard to do this, taking out maybe a quarter of the original manuscript. Dealing with lawyers at the new house, Viking, was much worse; we had some bad sessions, and I became very tenacious finally, anxious to hang onto everything in fear that I was being asked for the wrong reasons to take it out. The book's probably still informed a bit by that anxious tenacity.

LM: As you were developing the book, did you see your role as being, in any way, a vindicator of the Rosenbergs? I say this because it seemed pretty evident to me in reading the book that you felt the Rosenbergs were, if not completely innocent, then certainly not guilty enough to be executed.

RC: I originally felt back in 1966 that the execution of the Rosenbergs had been a watershed event in American history which we had somehow managed to forget or repress. I felt it was important to resurrect it and look at it again. By the time I'd finished researching the thing I was convinced, one, that they were not guilty as charged, and, two, even had they been, the punishment was hysterical and excessive. Indeed, given the macho arrogance of our military establishment, if anyone did contribute to the proliferation of information about the bomb, they probably did us all a favor. They were dead, there was no one to feel sorry for. I wasn't trying to vindicate them in that sense, but it was important that we remember it, that we not be so callous as to just shrug it off, or else it can happen again and again.

LM: Various reviewers used the term "apocalyptic" in describing the mood of this book. Is that accurate?

RC: No. Apocalypse is a magical idea borrowed from Christian mythology and the notion of cyclical time and a purpose in history. But short of apocalypse there's always disaster, which we have visited upon us from day to day. We have had, in that sense, an unending sequence of apocalypses, long before Christianity began and up to the present. From generation to generation, whole peoples get wiped from the face of the earth, so for them the apocalypse has already happened. And we can be pretty sure there's more to come. I mean, who can stop it? And technologically it's so much more frightening today. So in a lot of contemporary fiction there's a sense of foreboding disaster which is part of the times, just like self-reflexive fictions.

LM: Let's talk about what you are working on right now. When I met you seven or eight years ago, you were working on a long book called *Lucky Pierre,* which you were very excited about. Are you still engaged in that project?

RC: Yes, but other things have intervened. I've been working on theater pieces, radio plays, things like that. And shorter fictions. After the gigantism of *The Public Burning,* this is the year of the small book. Five of them, in fact. Viking is publishing one, *A Political Fable,* which originally appeared in 1968 as "The Cat in the Hat for President," and the other four are being done by small presses. Two of them, *After Lazarus* and *Hair o' the Chine,* are in the form of filmscripts, written nearly twenty years ago. The other two are new novella-length fictions, *Charlie in the House of Rue,* from Penmaen Press, and *Spanking the Maid,* which Bruccoli-Clark is publishing. And there's another novel-length fiction, not too long I hope, which is on my desk and walls right now, so *Lucky Pierre* will have to wait yet a bit longer. Impatient as he is, the restless fucker.

Interview, 1986

David Applefield

DA: Your work falls into a sphere that has critically become known as "metafiction" as opposed to this newer movement towards a fiction of hyper-realism à la Raymond Carver and followers which is dominating much of contemporary American fiction writing, especially the type that is taught or encouraged in university writing programs. What would you say is happening with these opposing tendencies in American fiction and how do you and your work fit in?

RC: The proliferation of those writing programs has been something of a disaster, a kind of parasitic growth on the college curriculum, once thought benign, now visibly threatening to universities and literature alike. English departments are losing their integrity and autonomy, literature is losing its variety, its distinctive voices. Divine madness does not go over in a workshop. These programs tend to be run by people who are themselves products of such programs, converts, as you might say, to the established cult of the workshop. Any workshop is apt to be homogenizing anyway, even at Brown where we struggle to be different. When you have a dozen people talking about a piece of new fiction, there's a tendency to narrow the discussion to the two or three things that everybody can agree to discuss without offending or baffling one another. So a piece of writing that's unique and difficult and different and perhaps slightly outrageous is apt to get burnished away by that kind of conversation in a workshop no matter how bright and inventing the people in the workshop are. And then you add to that a professional voice that is all too frequently trying to hone away the rough edges and what you get is not so much neo-realism but what is more properly called—and apparently people take it as a term in which they are proud—minimalism. That needn't equal the least common denominator, but all too often does. Raymond Carver, who in fact is a wonderful writer with a voice—even if minimalist—of his own, has become a sort of godfather, unwittingly I think, of this burgeoning school of workshop storywriters, all of whom sound more and more like one

From *Frank: An International Journal of Contemporary Writing and Art* (Paris), no. 6–7 (Winter-Spring 1987): 7–11.

another. As these people get their little degrees and spread about the country, they get control of literary magazines, even commercial magazines, in which with perhaps the best of intentions, they print one another. The more exciting and difficult writers, meanwhile, are often rejected from these writing programs or abandon them, fail then to get the influential jobs, lack access to these magazine staffs, and find themselves submitting their material to people who have been trained in what a "good story" is by way of these homogenizing workshops. Thus, there is a sense in which literature itself is being closed down by way of a narrow pathetically conservative vision of what narrative art is or can be.

DA: For someone who assigns a tremendous importance to innovation and intellectual wildness, how does the growing conservatism in America affect you and the observations that feed your work?

RC: Several things of course have been disturbing about the States. Unlike many of the people who suffered through it and have become disillusioned and disavowed, I think the 1960s was an incredibly rich and innovative time, although there were awful things happening. They were being met with a kind of innovativeness and imaginative resistance that spoke very well for the regenerative power of the United States. Or let's say, for the human race in general. That died. Crushed in some ways. Kent State was sort of a funeral termination of this moment of youth's best anarchical yea-saying in the face of calamity. And we sank back into something rather fearful and insecure. People became conscious of security and safety and of not rocking the boat. The years that passed have tended to create a feeling of malaise and vague unhappiness and a certain sense of futility. A response which is not that of the Sixties but that of the post Weimar Republic in Germany, a little bit vicious to put it in a word. I don't want to call it Nazi-like or fascistic, which are rather heavy history-laden words to apply to what is an essentially American phenomenon. The response to this kind of lingering malaise and uncertainty is to start whooping it up in a Fourth of July parade way. We have been going through the dark times and now the good times are coming. You hear it in country music; you hear it on all the TV fundamentalist religious programs; you see it in all the advertising; you hear it amongst the Yuppies, amongst the students at the universities at places like Brown, a kind of phoney macho optimism, all too often attached to some sort of mad ideology, in this case more often than not fundamentalist Christianity.

DA: Which is a subject that you've written about on several occasions.

RC: And I think I'm going back to it again. I thought the Sixties saw the end of a lot of things; it seemed to me that a lot of attitudes about the world were coming to an end, they were changing. They weren't necessarily going to change as dramatically as one would have hoped but they were going to be softened or ameliorated or altered in some way. The sexual revolution had taken place. There was a different attitude about relationships between men and women, between the races. This was the decade of the civil rights marches and there was a lot of joining of hands. It was true. You saw it right away. Now unexpectedly, that's vanishing. Some awful retreat has taken place. People, thought sane, have turned back to the supernatural, to magical thinking, to sleepwalking. So I feel like winding up the alarm again.

DA: You've spent a lot of time out of the United States. Several years in Spain, ten years in England. How has being outside of America affected your work and your vision?

RC: Up until the last part of *Gerald's Party* I could truthfully say that everything I had written I had written out of the country and after midnight. . . . Probably, if I didn't have to teach, I would still write better outside the country. Since I work so much from the outer structures inward, rather than from the inner out, I see things more clearly at a distance. Sometimes though, for specific details, I feel the need to get back home again, to watch TV, catch up on the jokes, hear people talk.

. . . .

DA: Farce has continually played a major role in your work. Do you find you have a hard time taking the world seriously?

RC: (laugh) (*Coover points to a sentence on the last page of his typescript "Cartoon"—"With a heavy heart [What a universe!]"*) I take life seriously in its details, I guess. Pain's pain, feelings are real, but my overview of the world is comic. I'm not going to laugh myself into a radioactive cloud, and I'll join in raising any kind of hell to stop it, but I'm not kidding myself that there's anything tragic about human craziness.

DA: But living in a world where extraordinary events occur—attacks on Libya, bombings here in Paris, nuclear accidents—how do you react to the news? . . . Do these events inform your work? How do you discern between the role of writer and the role of civilian?

RC: As a citizen, I act in the world as best I can, like anyone else. As a novelist, I suppose, among other things, I'm something of an iconoclast. Perhaps what most disturb and irritate me, though they are part of the comedy of course, are the brutalizing consequences of what you might call "the serious views of life"—the mad visions of those persons who do see life as having a profound meaning and their own individual lives as having some eternal role and who wish to impose all that on other people. This is what causes about 90 percent of our unnecessary pain. A lot of our pain is of course unavoidable, and quite enough to bear without inventing more.

DA: Is Ronald Reagan one of these persons?

RC: Yes, but what successful politician isn't? These people tend to rise to power by incarnating some sort of mad vision of the people. Politicians tend to be the most dangerous members of the society, often the craziest or most obsessed, at the very least the most opportunist. And often they do encapsulate those elements of society that are its most perverse and, as far as the rest of the world is concerned, dangerous. So, I think one of our most valuable and anarchical functions as writers is constantly to undermine the power of these people, if it's only by poking fun at them or making them look a bit ludicrous or vulnerable, somehow dissolving some of that magic that they tend to exercise. I do that formally too. One reason that my structures are themselves iconoclastic is that I worry about forms that get entrenched, dogmatized, and rigidified. Anything that becomes a rule begins to bother me. I begin to distrust it; it's probably going to end up causing more harm than good. I prefer a kind of ceaseless, pointless change, if it has to come to that, to any kind of rigidified ideals.

DA: You've been composing on a computer for about six years now. Has the computer changed things for you as a writer? The technology, clearly, creates changes in the way writers write. And biographers and bibliographers are faced with new challenges.

RC: I feel, with the computer, I write more efficiently now. And, if anything, I enjoy it more. It suits the kind of writing—and intensive rewriting—I've done more laboriously all along. As for bibliographers, my desire is to make it harder for them than ever. My idea is to create fluid texts, which are different each time they're ordered up. This could be done easily through the lifetime of a writer, but it could be done plotted out in such a way that it could last a long time afterwards whereby each time someone asked for a certain book under a certain title he'd get a slightly different book than the person who got it just before.

DA: If I can pose a classic interviewer's question . . . Can you name the thinkers, writers, or artists that have influenced you and your work considerably?

RC: The list changes each time I'm asked for it because recent reading has a way of blotting out what has happened earlier. The seminal, crucial and critical influence on me was Beckett at a moment when I needed conviction about myself as a writer in a vocational sense as opposed to a commercial or professional sense. And he also clarified for me, at least as I understood it at the time, where narrative art had drawn itself to, and what might be the ways out of it or beyond it. And I was reading lots of other people along the way who touched me in deep ways—Kafka, Joyce, Dostoevsky, Flaubert—people who don't seem to make a pattern. Few American writers had this effect on me. Melville did. Faulkner to a degree. Nabokov certainly, if we can claim him as an American. Hemingway struck me much like my reaction to the minimalist writers. A very good one. But I was angry about a lot of things in his work. I liked Henry Miller for his iconoclasm, and also William Burroughs, who was publishing just about the time I was beginning to do my first serious writing. Nathaniel West in a lesser way. Overrated but not uninteresting. Most American writing, though, especially the current favorites, left me cold. Pynchon, Hawkes, Elkin, Barth had not yet come along. I was reading Latin American writers early on, some of them before they were translated, people like Borges and Asturias, and Fuentes and Cortazar. The *nouveau roman* people. Grass and Calvino. When I think about what most altered my perceptions of the world and how to write stories, though, it tended not to be other fiction writers, so much as philosophers and historians and scientists. People like Freud and Durkheim and Kierkegaard and Kant and all the revisionist historians of the time. My graduate degree at Chicago was mainly in philosophy, though admittedly I was reading with a kind of wild unschematic randomness. I was just examining bookshelves and hauling things down and taking them home and sort of eating them up—it was really a kind of piecing together of the language that expressed the vision that I already had anyway and finding the linkages that held these kind of disparate notions of the world together. And I'm continually testing this out. One way you test out your vision of the world is to invent a story and play it through. And if something starts to ring false in it you try to make it true and in the process you learn something about that part of the world you're looking at; it might be part of yourself.

DA: Walker Percy, in his essay "The Diagnostic Novel" (*Harper's Magazine,* June 1986), states: "In short, any literature requires as the very condition of its life a certain consensus.... Now I think it fair to begin with the assumption, which seems fairly obvious, that ... the center is not holding; that the consensus ... is at least seriously called into question.... To judge from a good many contemporary novels, films, and plays, it often appears that the only consensus possible is a documentation of the fragmentation. The genre of meaninglessness has in fact become the chic property not only of the café existentialist but even of Hollywood." Percy then goes on to affirm that the modern world has ended and thus justifies his call for a new literature. Do you agree with his impulse?

RC: He's asking what the function of literature is in a time like this? Well, I agree with the perception, a perception I had when I began writing 30 years ago, a perception common to all generations, I think, that one era is ending and a new one's about to begin. It's kind of a cliché in intellectual history. Often it takes the Joachimite form of three ages—the past age which is defined in lots of ways, then its contrary also defined in lots of ways, and finally the transcendent third age which, not surprisingly, is always just about to happen. An unlikely story, but one I've borrowed on occasion for the sake of irony. I think there is something to be said though for the notion that we seem to be in a kind of transitional time intellectually. I don't see it as catastrophic or even mysterious or even as an age to be regretted. I think it's just something that's happening and it's okay. I think that the Enlightenment, which Percy likes to equate with modern Christiandom, was founded on an essentially Aristotelian view of the world—we've come to the end of that quite a long time ago. Progress, history, science, the comfortable Newtonian vision of the Universe, language itself in its hopeful definitions and dreams of precision, have all let us down, and we have been thrown into a time of randomness and rhetoric that might be thought of as classically Sophist. Sophism is a less secure vision of the world than those we've enjoyed under Christiandom. Plato hated it. He saw the Sophists living in the world of "Becoming" without understanding his visionary world of "Being." And that's exactly right. A good Sophist would say there is no such place, this is just fantasizing on the part of Platonists and that Platonists in fact close the world down with their insistence that they know what that thing looks like or ought to. To hell with them, we are living in a world of "Becoming" and that's all we've

117

got. Well, that conviction need not cause despair. Though it alters the way we communicate with one another, it doesn't necessarily mean that something terrible is happening or something monstrous is about to be born. It's more likely that we'll simply have more of the same under a new disguise, new forms of arguments. Platonists and Aristotelians and scientific types don't die; they just hang in, awaiting a change in the intellectual fashion. Now, concerning the way dialogue is exchanged, it is true that there's a large sense of "the center not holding" (which has become a cliché in our time)—I mean the center has probably never ever held. It certainly wasn't holding in Cervantes' day and what happened as Cervantes lived and died was not a world catastrophe, yet there was a good case made at the time that the center was not holding and the vision of the world was changing. Quixote's sad march out into the world was an expression in a tragicomic way of the center having failed to hold and something new being born to which one could not yet give a name. In the end the name of the particular literary form was the novel, but that was another hundred years to come. So, I think we are in that sort of time. And literature has the function it always has; it continues to reflect the realities of its time. And this is what I've often found wrong with conventional forms. They do not successfully do that; they reconstruct through their forms the realities of a past time that aren't with us any more. They rebuild by the way they put their books together that lost structure. I think what novelists who are true realists do is to reflect reality in their forms, to imitate in their forms reality as they see it. And what they see is something like what Percy's describing. It's as though he's been, if I may say so, to *Gerald's Party*.

Interview, 1989

Thomas E. Kennedy

The interview that follows was conducted by post. At first, Mr. Coover was "cool to the idea."

"I'm tired of interviews, aren't you?" he wrote. "I talk so much inside my fictions, I can't really see the point of prolonging the talk outside of them unless it's just to provoke me to say badly what I've already said more or less well." But in the course of further correspondence, he agreed to answer a few questions, and the result was the following interview—a useful aid, I think, to contemplating the mechanics of Coover's brilliant, complex, and entertaining short fiction.

The completed version of the interview that Mr. Coover originally sent me was destroyed by the Postal Service; fortunately, Mr. Coover kept copies of his replies. The replacement copy concluded with this sad note: "Mr. Kennedy: This is a reprint of the earlier letter, Barthelme remarks now sadly in past tense. When answering your questions, I had thought of it as a dialogue with Donald."

TK: In his two collections, *Sixty Stories* (1981) and *Forty Stories* (1987), Donald Barthelme chose the word *stories* for the titles—not *fictions, ficciones, tales,* or *fictoids,* but *stories.* He defines story as "a process of accretion. Barnacles growing on a wreck or a rock. I'd rather have a wreck than a ship that sails. Things attach themselves to wrecks. Strange fish find your wreck or rock to be a good feeding ground."[1] How would you define a story?

RC: Descriptive terms for prose narratives are all undermined somewhat by the ambiguous, paradoxical, and ironical nature of the form itself. "New novel" and "postmodernism" are two of the more comical examples of this. I used "fictions" at a time when "stories" was the more common term to emphasize what I felt to be uncommon about my formal notions and to make a bridge with the remote past. Donald Barthelme, deeper ironist that he was, used the popular term as that which would least describe what he was doing, allowing the ironies to accrue as might barnacles, to coin an image, to a wreck. This definition of story as "a process of accretion" applies, I think, to all his narratives equally, long and short.

TK: The majority of your books are novels, but your short fiction clearly has had an enormous impact on the fiction being written in the United States over the past twenty years. You have said that stories appear to you not as formal ideas but as metaphors that seem to demand structures of their own and have an internal need for a certain form. Do they also have the need for a certain genre? A certain length? I am wondering here about the relationship between the two treatments of Nixon: the big novel, *The Public Burning*, and the short one, *What Ever Happened to Gloomy Gus*. Also, I am wondering about the various factors, internal and external, that have you writing shorter fiction at certain periods, longer at others. And more specifically, the fictions in *Pricksongs & Descants* tend to be of about standard length for American short stories whereas the pieces in *In Bed One Night & Other Brief Encounters* are for the most part of a prose-poem length. Then again, *Spanking the Maid* is novella-length, although a short-story-sized segment of it appeared in *Best American Short Stories 1981*.

RC: To pursue Barthelme's metaphor, whereas the length of his fictions depends more upon the appetitiveness of the barnacles and his passing fascination with strange fish, the length of mine would depend more upon the size and lingering power of the structural wreck that has to be eaten. His bemused and foundered wreck would contemplate with wry delight its barnacles; my blind barnacle would try, in that hysterical moment before something ate *it*, to intuit the full enormity of the wreck upon which, as though condemned, it fed. If nothing but a stone after all, a simple splinter, it would soon move on, else stay forever as forevers go. I do not, then, go through "periods," as you suggest, but gnaw away at many wrecks at once, some dissolving at the first bite, others never to be finished.

Thus, too, for me, as belabored here, the compelling nature of metaphor itself, infinitely fecund source of most, perhaps all, my fictions. I start, not with characters or situations, abstract ideas or social issues, but with what Italo Calvino calls "an image that for some reason strikes me as charged with meaning, even if I cannot formulate this meaning in discursive or conceptual terms." What remains hidden under analytical scrutiny reveals itself within narrative flow, the images themselves developing, as Calvino goes on to say, "their own implicit potentialities, the story they carry within them."[2] It is this, then, the story within, that determines length, that and one's intransigence in the pursuit of its full revelation, not always unfaltering even in the most willing of servants.

TK: A question that has always intrigued me is the extent to which a fiction, a story, can be accessible. How fully can a story be understood? To what degree is the intellect per se involved in a story? More specifically, how fully and at what stage in the writing process do you "understand" your own fictions? Do you ever "see" a turn in a piece without knowing why, only that it is right? How great a role does intuition play in your work? Do your characters ever lead the way when you write, as Forster said his did in the *Passage to India*, or are they, as Nabokov claimed his to be, reacting to Forster, "galley slaves" who do what they are told?[3]

RC: After the surrender, the Nabokovian exploration, all faculties engaged, cold reason not excluded, nor hot either. Intuition might be just a bad guess, after all, a wayward character, a perverse distraction, watch out. Structures, once perceived, can then be thought about, thoughts tested, perceptions refined, structures honed and elaborated, or abandoned altogether. Nevertheless, that said: yes, the text and its metaphors do sometimes lead the way. Inner forces emerging from the narrative itself, whether as rebellious "characters" or the "spontaneous" eruption of event and imagery, are more to be trusted in the end than rational design, no matter how ingeniously contrived. Calvino, after insisting on the importance of orderly, discursive thought in the shaping of a narrative, goes on to say: "Yet the visual solutions continue to be determining factors and sometimes unexpectedly come to decide situations that neither the conjectures of thought, nor the resources of language would be capable of resolving."[4] There are many scenes in my work which I did not "write," but rather, in a sense, allowed to be written. Quite likely, though I am no judge, they are the best ones: moments when unanticipated actions swept over me, language announced itself, or characters took matters in their own hands. Over twenty years ago Henry Waugh was already perplexed and fascinated by this strange, yet somehow delicious phenomenon. A universal experience, I think. See Edward Gorey's *The Unstrung Harp, or, Mister Earbrass Writes a Novel.*

TK: The current movement in American fiction seems to be away from experiment, innovation, metafiction, and back to realism. The British periodical *Granta* characterizes contemporary American fiction as "Dirty Realism" and, in a follow-up presentation of same, "More Dirt."[5] The third edition of *The Norton Anthology of Short Fiction* has purged its pages of innovators like Barth, Barthelme, and Mark Costello and replaced them with pieces by Raymond Carver, James Alan McPherson, and Bobbie Ann

Mason. How do you feel about this, what *American Book Review* has called the "backward turning of American literary taste?"[6]

RC: I have answered the historical question at such length elsewhere, it seems pointless to repeat myself here, other than to point out that a fundamental change took place in all the arts, high and low, after World War II, achieving a kind of public climax in the 1960s. A different world view had been generated by physics, history, technology, medicine, cultural encounter, space flight, what-all, and the changing art forms all over the world reflected that: thus, those of us who participated in that movement were less innovators than true children of our own time, and those who ignored it and ignore it still are increasingly irrelevant and oblivion-bound. Nor can they be called "realists," dirty or otherwise. (The old forms are not completely dead, of course; though no longer of any interest artistically, they remain useful sociologically and therapeutically.)

TK: The new American studies programs, which have been combining the study of literature, sociology, and history, have begun to turn from the reading of "texts" to the reading of buildings, neon "crafts," fairs, department stores, and garbage. Some proponents of American studies spurn literature, particularly the classics, as "elitist" and turn instead to the "cultural geography" of the streets. What are your thoughts about this?

RC: They are, given the nature of their quests, quite right. Literature, like all arts, is completely useless. It is only, sometimes, like other great high-wire acts, daringly beautiful.

TK: Your fiction has a kind of Chaucerian celebration of the vulgar that is wonderfully comic, particularly in its contrast to the high tone of the prose you sometimes choose to surround it with—a little like Jung's story from his childhood of experiencing great anxiety every time he looked upon the great Cathedral of Bern, until finally he let himself go, let the anxiety break open to reveal a vision of a great turd dropping from the heavens to smash the cathedral's roof, thus balancing the high and low for him.[7]

RC: Life tends toward either tedium or melodrama, none of it reassuring. "Ah, the horror, the horror," as Stanley Elkin has said somewhere. Religion has always seemed to me an insane defense against that, comedy a saner one, though a defense just the same.

I might add that whenever I find one of my characters saying something like this, I usually try to kill him off . . . .

Notes

1. Donald Barthelme, interviewed by Larry McCaffery in *Anything Can Happen: Interviews with Contemporary American Novelists*, ed. Tom Le Clair and Larry McCaffrey (Urbana: University of Illinois Press), 321.

2. Italo Calvino, quoted by Coover in interview.

3. See part 1, *Pricksongs & Descants*, note 6.

4. Calvino, quoted by Coover.

5. See Part 1, "Introduction," note 7.

6. Lance Olsen, "The Charnel Imp," in *American Book Review* 9, no. 6 (January-February 1988): 12.

7. See part 1, *A Night at the Movies*, note 4.

Part 3

THE CRITICS

Introduction

In part 1 I incorporated into my own review the views, pro and con, of some critics about the short fiction of Robert Coover. Also useful, however, are the following longer excerpts from a cross-sampling of other critics.

Most notably, I have included almost verbatim William Gass's historic review of Coover's *Pricksongs & Descants*, which first appeared in the *New York Times Book Review* and was reprinted shortly thereafter in his wonderful book *Fiction and the Figures of Life*. Gass was a very important figure in the fiction and criticism that achieved prominence in the 1960s and 1970s, and he recognized Coover's genius immediately. Because *Pricksongs & Descants* is, in my opinion, such an important book, I thought it also appropriate to include segments of the reviews of it by Joyce Carol Oates and Susan Kissel as well as Neil Schmitz's less than favorable comments on "the hazards of metafiction."

I find *Charlie in the House of Rue* particularly intriguing; because I do not deal with it at great length in part 1, I thought it useful to include a snatch of Jon Zonderman's review as well as Charla Gabert's longer view of that novella when it appeared in book form in 1980, seven years before its incorporation into *A Night at the Movies*.

Finally, I have selected an excerpt from Caryn James's review of *In Bed One Night & Other Brief Encounters*, since my own treatment of that slender volume is itself rather slender, and a brief statement by John O'Brien on the novella *Spanking the Maid*, which I have not dealt with in my study.

I believe that this sampling of excerpts will supplement and counterbalance my own opinions on Coover's short fiction and those of the other critics dealt with in the part 1.

William H. Gass on *Pricksongs & Descants*

...Most of the fictions in Robert Coover's remarkable volume are soli-taires—sparkling, many-faceted.[1] Sharply drawn and brightly painted paragraphs are arranged like pasteboards in ascending or descending scales of alternating colors to compose the story, and the impression that we might scoop them all up and reshuffle, altering not the elements but the order or the rules of play, is deliberate. We are led to feel that a single fable may have various versions: narrative time may be disrupted (the ten played before the nine), or the same space occupied by different eyes (jack of hearts or jack of diamonds), fantasy may fall on fact, lust overnumber love, cliché cover consternation. The characters are highly stylized like the face cards. We've had them in our hands before: Swede, the taciturn guide; Quenby, his island-lonely wife; Ola, their nubile daughter; Carl, the fish-erman out from the city...and in other stories there are others equally standardized, equally traditional.

Just like the figures in old fairy tales and fables, we are constantly com-ing to forks in the road (always fateful), except here we take all of them, and our simultaneous journeys are simultaneous stories, yet in different genres, sometimes different styles, as if fantasy, romance and reality, nightmare and daydream, were fingers on the same hand. In "The Eleva-tor," several types of self-serviced trips are imagined for its fourteen floors plus B, and the fact that the story is in fifteen numbered paragraphs seems as inevitable as the fourteen lines of the sonnet.

One of the most impressive pieces in the book in this regard is called "The Babysitter." She arrives at seven-forty, but how will her evening be? ordinary? the Tucker children bathed and put away like dishes, a bit of TV, then a snooze? Or will she take a tub herself, as she seems to have done the last time? Will she, rattled, throttle the baby to silence its screaming, allow it to smother in sudsy water? Perhaps her boyfriend will drop over for a spot of love? and bring a sadistic friend? Or maybe a mysterious stranger will forcibly enter and enter her? No—she will seduce the children; no—they will seduce her; no—Mr. Tucker, with the ease and suddenness of daydream, will return from the party and (a) surprise her in carnal con-

From *Fiction and the Figures of Life* (New York: Vintage, 1972), 104–9; originally pub-lished in *New York Times Book Review*.

junction with her boyfriend, (b) embrace her slippery body in the bath, (c) be discovered himself by (i) his wife, (ii) his friends, (iii) the police . . . or . . . All the while the TV has its own tale to tell, and eventually, perhaps, on the news, an account will be given of . . . While the baby chokes on its diaper pin? While the sitter, still warm from the water, is taken by Mr. Tucker? While both she and the children are murdered by Boyfriend & Friend? No . . . But our author says yes to everything; we've been reading a remarkable fugue—the stock fears and wishes, desires and dangers of our time done into Bach.

Within the paragraphs, the language, which is artfully arranged and colored for both eye and ear, reads often like a scene set for the stage:

Night on the lake. A low cloud cover. The boat bobs silently, its motor for some reason dead.

Or it has the quality of an image on the oblong screen which is being described for us because we've been carried away into the kitchen and yet wish to miss nothing: what's happening now, dear?

Mark is kissing her. Jack is under the blanket, easing her panties down over her squirming hips.

The present tense is often salted with a sense of something altogether over.

I wander the island, inventing it. I make a sun for it, and trees—pines and birch and dogwood and firs—and cause the water to lap the pebbles of its abandoned shores.

While the collection is dominated by the paragraph as playing card, there are short pseudo dramas and sections of monologue, too, as well as patches of more traditional narrative, for this is a book of virtuoso exercises: alert, self-conscious, instructional, and show-off. Look at me, look at me, look at me now, says the Cat in the Hat. Indeed, Coover is the one to watch—a marvelous magician—as the last piece, "The Hat Act," suggests; a maker of miracles, a comic, a sexual tease, befooler of the hicks and ultimately a vain rebuilder of Humpty Dumpty, murderer of his own muse, a victim of his own art . . . mastered by it, diddled, tricked, rendered powerless by the very power he possesses as an artist:

At times, I forget that this arrangement is my own invention. I begin to think of the island as somehow real, its objects solid and intractable, its condition of ruin not so much an aesthetic design as an historical denouement. I find myself peering into blue teakettles, batting at spider-webs, and contemplating a greenish-gray growth on the side of a stone parapet. I wonder if others might wander here without my knowing it; I wonder if I might die and the teakettle remain.... Where does this illusion come from, this sensation of "hardness" in a blue teakettle ... ?

A number of our finest writers—Barth, Coover, and Barthelme, for example—have begun to experiment with shorter forms, as Beckett and Borges before them, and in many ways each wishes to instruct us in the art of narration, the myth-making imagination. The regions they have begun to develop are emphatically not like the decaying South, the Great Plains, or the Lower East Side; they are rather regions of the mind, aspects of a more or less mass college culture; and therefore the traditions—the experience—they expect to share with their readers is already largely "literary" ... [deleted text] biblical stories, fairy tales, and the myths and fables of popular culture most concern Coover in the short pieces he's collected here, as well as in some others which he has yet to reprint.

... [deleted text] Coover rewrites Little Red Riding Hood (and who is the woodman but Beanstalk Jack?); gives us a beautiful new Hansel and Gretel; adds to our knowledge of Joseph and Mary (how did he take it?); injects as much bitterness as flood into the story of Noah; leans toward goatboy allegory in a tale titled "Morris in Chains," etc., and at all times contrives to counter, even to destroy, the meaning and power of the original.

Coover himself remarks, in a dedicatory preface addressed to Cervantes and placed with predictable perverseness well within the body of the book, that

> The novelist uses familiar mythic or historical forms to combat the content of those forms and to conduct the reader ... to the real, away from mystification to clarification, away from magic to maturity, away from mystery to revelation.

No wonder, then, that in the tale about the Ark, it's not the high and dry Coover writes about, but the abandoned, the drowned.

It is finally significant, I think, that the experimental methods which interest Coover, and which he chooses to exploit so skillfully, are those which have to do with the orderly, objective depiction of scenes and events, those which imply a world with a single public point of view, solid and enduring things, long strings of unambiguous action joined by tight causal knots, even when the material itself is improbable and fantastic; and the consequence of his play with these techniques is the scrambling of everything, the dissolution of that simple legendary world we'd like to live in, in order that new values may be voiced; and, as Coover intends them, these stories become "exemplary adventures of the Poetic Imagination."

It is also characteristic of this kind of writing to give covert expression to its nature, provide its own evaluation; so that the imagined reader, dressed in red riding, bringing a basket to her wolf-enclosed granny and hesitating momentarily before the cover of the cottage, finally opens the door with the thought

> that though this was a comedy from which, once entered, you never returned, it nevertheless possessed its own astonishments and conjurings, its tower and closets, and even more pathways, more gardens, and more doors.

This reader, too, will subscribe to that.

Note

1. My ellipses. Unless otherwise indicated, all other ellipses appeared in Gass's original text and do not signify deleted text.

Joyce Carol Oates on *Pricksongs & Descants*

In *Pricksongs & Descants* Coover . . . exists blatantly and brilliantly . . . as an authorial consciousness, not at all interested in creating old-fashioned worlds for us to believe in, but interested—obsessed, rather—in creating a dimension of personality that is pure style, pure eloquence, "form" equalling "content." . . . [B]oth crude and intellectual, predictable and alarming, he gives the impression of thoroughly enjoying his craft.

Coover's art is the kind that can move gracefully into pure drama, pure imagined drama, and it is significant that the last item in *Pricksongs & Descants* is a bizarre short play, "The Hat Act," reminiscent of Ionesco's early one-act plays. Action begins ordinarily enough, then accelerates to madness; it is always mysterious, always inexplicable, and yet its ending comes at exactly the right time. Coover is in charge of the "hat act," a formidable magician. At the end he declares the act "concluded" and regrets that there will be no refund. This act—and the other acts of the book—are extremely entertaining, but entertaining in a coolly intellectual way. We cannot

From "Realism of Distance, Realism of Immediacy," *Southern Review* 8, no. 1 (Winter 1971).

become emotionally involved because there are no emotions in the stories; there are familiar responses, the parodies of normal emotional responses, and the shapes of familiar people come and go, along with the shapes—the sounds—of familiar human dialogue. And yet it is not human: it is magic.

Susan Kissel on *Pricksongs & Descants*

[In the story "The Hat Act," the] metaphor of the failing magician is a powerful one through which Coover suggests both the comedy of the artist's perspiring efforts to please and the horror of his possible failure to control his art; if he cannot master the techniques of his evolving craft, both the artist and his audience, it is clear, will experience fearful losses.

Coover suggests that the contemporary artist—bound as he is to his audience as performer, magician, and funhouse designer, and sensitive as he must be to the expectations and desires of those he entertains—nevertheless must not let his readers exert ultimate control over his efforts. Instead, Coover indicates that the contemporary artist must often find himself disappointing his audience—disappointing himself in fact—as in "Romance of the Thin Man and the Fat Lady" where, in responding to the "precious metaphor" of the circus couple's relationship, the narrator reveals "we are irritated to discover their limits, to find that the Ludicrous is not also Beautiful. . . . Well, let us admit it, perhaps it is ourselves who are corrupted. Perhaps we have seen or been too many Ringmasters, watched too many parades, safely witnessed too many thrills, counted through too many books. Maybe it's just that we've lost a taste for the simple in a world perplexingly simple" (p. 52).

To help his audience regain a taste for the perplexing possibilities inherent in the simple story, Coover repeatedly explores the basic myths of our cultural heritage and restores to these familiar stories the horror, irony, and comedy of their age-old human dramas: of Little Red Riding Hood in "The Door"; of Hanzel and Gretel in "The Gingerbread House"; of Noah's Ark in "The Brother"; and of the Virgin Birth in "J's Marriage" (as well as in *A Theological Position* from the collection of plays which bears its title). These simple stories of human betrayal, human misery, and human desire reveal

From "The Contemporary Artist and His Audience in the Short Stories of Robert Coover," *Studies in Short Fiction* 16, no. 1 (Winter 1979): 52–54.

Coover's premise that the fiction writer can only repeat the past and repeat himself, however cleverly.

Robert Coover knows all too well that the simple story, however viewed, will not satisfy the experienced tastes of the modern audience. In "Klee Dead," for instance, the narrator admits that his "show" has been "Pretty dull stuff." . . . [He] reminds the reader that the writer is limited to the basic human experience in his fantasies and myths and that the stories to be found there will not astound or shock or uplift with their familiarity. Fiction can provide only a lesser stimulation in our amusement-oriented culture. The narrator's ironic offer of circus tickets in "Klee Dead" . . . comments upon the modern reader's insatiable appetite for novelty and sensation in arm-chair entertainment—an appetite which the reader shares with the much less sophisticated circus and street crowds he disdains.

The picture Robert Coover creates of the modern audience, then, is not always a flattering one; he suggests that the contemporary literary audience, with its intelligent, sophisticated readership, is guilty of the mass audience's exploitive, hostile demands for entertainment. . . . And yet Coover implies that the artist cannot afford to please his disappointed audience with new, bizarre tricks, without finally destroying the whole show and becoming, himself, the monster-magician dragged off the stage at the end of "The Hat Act." . . .

Neil Schmitz on *Pricksongs & Descants*

For Coover the presence of [the] demystified narrator (I invent, I make, I cause) is invariably comic; he is Prospero in a blazer and ascot, a fumbling magician, the tyrannical moderator of a TV panel show. He is also Coover's fate and that recognition often makes the comedy desperate. In *Pricksongs & Descants*, his most representative work to date, he writes variously in both moods and reveals at every turn the paradoxical nature of this particular approach to fiction. In such metafictive art, Fredric Jameson notes [in "Metacommentary," *PMLA*, January, 1971], "it is wrong to want to *decide*, to want to *resolve* a difficulty." What is exhibited is not objective content but a "mental procedure which suddenly shifts gears, which throws

From "Robert Coover and the Hazards of Metafiction," *Novel: A Forum on Fiction 7*, no. 4 (Spring 1974): 210–19. Reprinted with permission.

Part 3

everything in an inextricable tangle one floor higher, and turns the very problem itself (the obscurity of this sentence) into its own solution (the varieties of Obscurity) by widening its frame in such a way that it now takes in its own mental processes as well as the object of those processes" (pp. 210–11).

[If] Beckett's trilogy, *Molloy, Malone Dies* and *The Unnameable*, is in effect a single sentence, the unbroken chronicle of an austere intelligence painstakingly articulating the motion of its consciousness, Coover's metafiction is principally directed elsewhere—toward the technique of writing, toward fiction as a game of choices, and not toward writing as metaphysical risk-taking. What is for Beckett a point of departure for some purer form of meditational discourse is for Coover a formal and stylistic *cul de sac*. The final story in *Pricksongs & Descants*, "The Hat Act," comically pre-figures the frustrated toil in Coover's recent story . . . "Beginnings." In "The Hat Act" an exemplary magician, a lower-case version of the Beckett-like sculptor, fails to extricate the warm breathing body of a woman from his hat, but gives us nonetheless the performance of his incapacity, his desperate striving. In "Beginnings" Coover takes drastic measures to rid himself of the obtrusive narrator, the I writing: "In order to get started, he went to live alone on an island and shot himself." But the writer-hero resolutely survives to share the magician's fate. His narrative is a sequence of enveloped fictions, pluckings from the hat of invention. The tone in both stories is ambivalent, darkly humorous. Coover writes in such a way as to suggest that the liberation from content (plot and character) frees the writer for nothing. Where Beckett is intensely present in his narrative voice, Coover is not (pp. 211–12).

Jon Zonderman on *Charlie in the House of Rue*

Robert Coover has turned Chaplin on his head. In *Charlie in the House of Rue* Coover has placed the Little Tramp in a house where his timing, no matter how perfect, can not draw from the other characters the slightest response.

At first, the Tramp is merely annoyed by this. But Coover doesn't just pose for us the "what if nobody responded" question. He goes a step further and sets the supporting characters on their own courses.

From *American Book Review* 4, no. 2 (January–February 1982): 24.

The beautiful woman, whom the Tramp is mystified and made humble by, tries to commit suicide. While attempting to keep her from her course—jumping off the top of the staircase—the Tramp accidentally pushes her over the edge, where she dangles by the rope around her neck while he scampers around the foyer and second storey trying to get her down. Even Charlie grabbing for his baggy pants to keep them up, then his derby to keep it on, then his pants, then his derby, pants, derby, pants, derby, can't bring humor to this grisly scene.

The bald man, yes, the ubiquitous bald man with the thick mustache and suspenders, whose pate is used for everything, including an ashtray, gives the Tramp his comeuppance by standing at the kitchen table, looking into the soup that he has been sullenly staring at throughout the story, and promptly urinating into it. . . .

The lights are always going out on the Tramp, and he finds himself in a place he never thought he'd be. He strikes the man, only to find it is the woman. . . . By the three-quarter point of the book, the story is moving at breakneck speed, yet there is no more slapstick to the pratfalls. It is no longer Chaplin, not even Olson and Johnson.

Once again, Coover has created a character beyond the edge, one who has taken his lunacy to the point where it turns on him. . . .

The thread that runs through all Coover's work is the notion of America gone haywire, the fiercely independent character, always in control, suddenly out of control, no longer a part of the world around him. In Coover's world, not only do Americans have no history, but no reality. They are merely the lines of type in a newspaper, the statistics in a baseball record book and, finally, fleeting images on a moving-picture screen.

Charla Gabert on *Charlie in the House of Rue*

Charlie in the House of Rue is a miniature tragicomedy which takes as its point of departure the character and conventions of a Charlie Chaplin film. . . . As the story progresses, however, we are drawn away from our preconceptions about a Chaplinesque Charlie and into the dream-like, funhouse world of Coover.

From "The Metamorphosis of Charlie," *Chicago Review* 32, no. 2 (Autumn 1980): 60–64. ©1980 *Chicago Review*.

Part 3

The aesthetic problem of translating literature into the medium of film is a commonly discussed one, but Coover's opposite task is equally difficult and interesting. . . . Coover's words create the texture of a silent Charlie Chaplin movie.

The text preserves certain formal aspects of film: visually precise rendering of actions, sudden shifts in scene, and the juxtaposition of ostensibly unrelated images. Coover utilizes only the present tense to simulate the immediacy of a live performance—of things seen rather than told—and to divorce the action from any antecedents or future results. Written in a consistently descriptive prose, the text captures physical motion with the same precise, literal accuracy that a camera does. Sentences are rhythmically related to the movements they refer to, ranging from short and curt to long and breathless. "He stands, brushes himself off, smiles apologetically up at the lady, sets the vase back gently on the balustrade, mops his brow, straightens his tie, leans back in exhaustion, and knocks the vase to the tiled floor, where it shatters in a thousand pieces." Or: "He waves at her. He jumps up and down. He throws her a kiss." Since virtually all the action of the story is physical, Coover varies his prose to differentiate movements and to break the activity into meaningful units. In so doing, he emphasizes not only the visual quality of a silent film, but also the underlying pacing and tempo that are fundamental to all films—the rhythm that is created by the movements of the camera, the length of each shot or scene in relation to the whole, and the repetition of discrete images or motifs.

The unique characteristics of silent films—absence of dialogue, and exaggerated gestures approaching pantomime—particularly dominate our expectations and shape the text. Charlie's psychological isolation and the primitive level of communication with other characters are economically expressed by the absence of speech, resulting in the impression that the "house of rue" is really a soundless vacuum. Coover has also drawn upon familiar conventions of horror film to reiterate the connection of his text to film: the shot of an emaciated white hand emerging from a coffin to push back the lid; the idea of a victim trapped in a house that is actively hostile; the silent scream which cannot be heard and is terrifying for that reason.

Although most of the familiar elements of a Chaplin film are on display—Chaplin as comic victim and mischievous prankster, the slapstick antics of a well-intentioned but clumsy buffoon, the pretty but unapproachable girl—the crucial element of humor is missing. . . . Without the laugh to cushion his fall, Charlie gets hurt; without the humor to win us over, Charlie looks malicious.

The narrator's voice is, for Coover, unusually circumspect and unobtrusive. In his earlier work of short fictions, *Pricksongs and Descants,* Coover did not hesitate to emphasize the author's controlling, inventive role and to point to the choices involved in the creative act. The multiplicity of overlapping, contradictory events, and the prismatic quality of the plots, required the presence of a self-consciously inventive narrator, who proclaimed his arbitrary power and worked to subvert the idea that a single reality was being portrayed. In *Charlie in the House of Rue,* however, Coover defines the narrator's role in terms of the passive, uniquely cinematic act of viewing. . . . Although Coover tracks a linear, narrative course through a kaleidoscopic series of events—which are related thematically rather than causally—the narrator's complete separation from the internal thoughts and feelings of his characters allows him to function as a "speculative spectator," who reads motives and meanings into Charlie's gestures and facial expressions much as a movie audience would do. The traditional concept of the narrator as a storyteller with some degree of insight into his characters recedes in importance; what replaces it is the viewpoint of an observer who watches and records events (over which he has no acknowledged control) as they unfold.

The nature of the events in *Charlie in the House of Rue* suggests, in fact, that no one is in control, least of all Charlie, who bounces from room to room like a pinball, buffeted by his own fears and desires, as well as by the constantly shifting rooms, objects and people. Assembled from a cast of easily identifiable stock figures, the people he encounters are little more than cartoon characters who function symbolically, almost allegorically—the policeman representing ineffectual authority, the sexually aggressive maid unbridled lust. These characters present us with no past or future, primarily because they cannot and do not speak. Their silence locks them into a reality that is visually compelling but ontologically empty; their actions are stylized, obsessive, and redundant. Each character exists in a separate realm—maid in the bedroom, woman in white in the foyer—while Charlie shuttles between them; when they vanish from Charlie's sight, they seem to disappear altogether. As the story progresses, they lose any semblance of being independent actors, and by the end, they are simply part of the hostile environment. Initially indifferent and unresponsive to Charlie, they grow increasingly aggressive, and attack him or try to thwart him. But even these actions resemble motiveless, gratuitous acts that are prompted not by their feelings or personal reactions to Charlie, but by an inexplicable stimulus outside of them.

Part 3

The surreal environment that exists inside the house is a landscape littered with dreamlike symbols, objects that change into something else at their own volition. Charlie throws a pie into an old man's face, but the face turns out to belong to the mournful woman in white, the last person Charlie wants to injure; her eyes are actually the old man's, but they soon metamorphose into the maid's bare behind.... As the chaos grows more violent around him, Charlie too becomes more frantic in his futile effort to gain control of the unpredictable activity threatening to engulf him.

The "house of rue" exists solely as an interior space, a world unto itself which is as claustrophobic as a sound stage. The space is never defined clearly; doors and rooms disappear and materialize as Charlie leaves and enters them. His presence in the house is never explained, his entrance is never recorded, but it is clear from the beginning that the house is an alien environment in which he is first an intruder, then a prisoner. As a metaphor for the psyche, the house contains the forces that Charlie unintentionally sets in motion as a prisoner of his own fears and desires, which the house's inhabitants merely reflect and exemplify. The concept of rue refers not only to the remorse and regret that Charlie feels for accidentally causing the woman in white to be hanged, but also to his growing recognition of himself as a moral force, someone who is not only sorry but who must suffer for his sins.

The contradiction between the other characters' initial indifference to Charlie and their subsequent hostility toward him suggests that they are emissaries sent to punish Charlie; it is not only internal guilt, but external retribution that he cannot escape. Indeed, the house is like a Kafkaesque torture chamber in which Charlie unwittingly finds himself judged, declared guilty, and punished, without even realizing that charges have been brought against him (pp. 60–63).

The last half of the story follows Charlie's desperate, ineffectual efforts to save the woman in white. As she dangles in the foyer, Charlie careens from room to room, searching for something to cut the rope (p. 63).

Charlie's progress from a state of playful innocence to one of fatal tragedy proceeds inexorably, despite his ostensibly random movement from one room, one situation, to the next. In confronting his own cruelty, he forfeits his familiar status as the eternal victim and assumes the role of victimizer. At the same time, as he falls prey to forces beyond his control and suffers the guilt of the woman's death, we see him as a modern antihero who lacks the resources to shape his own destiny. It is here, in the expansion of Charlie's character from the pathetic to the tragic, that Coover most clearly departs from the "Little Tramp" character. By the time we reach the conclusion, the sentimental ending of the silver screen will no longer suffice. Instead, Coover gives us Charlie clinging in mid-air to the woman's corpse as the lights go out around him—a black-humored inversion of a typical ending in which Charlie and the girl are finally united, then plunged into eternal darkness by the shrinking circle of the lens (p. 64).

Caryn James on *In Bed One Night & Other Brief Encounters*

Robert Coover's stories are mind games with a heart. *In Bed One Night & Other Brief Encounters* humanizes language games and literary theorizing, and, remarkably, does so by using cartoonish characters and a nearly anonymous narrative voice. While these nine very short pieces don't amount to much in themselves, they are miniature demonstrations of the control Coover displays in his more substantial work. Like a literary juggler, he keeps all the parts of his fiction in motion, balancing rhythm, word play, and the central image of the author creating his story. Or does the story create the author?

"Beginnings," written in 1972, masterfully explores this question. "In order to get started, he went to live alone on an island and shot himself," reads the first line. What he starts is the story we're reading. . . . This circular undercutting of cause and effect is the most facile part of "Beginnings." Reaching for substance, Coover brings the author-character to life, making him implausible, mundane, unique, and universal. The island becomes a postlapsarian Eden, complete with Eve (this time she's the one who gives up a rib), children, and the distractions and rewards of family life. . . .

Though the more recent works are slighter, they share some characteristic Coover effects. "Here's what happened it was pretty good" is the first line of "An Encounter." "The Old Man" starts, "This one has to do with an old man." Such stories belong to the second generation of metafiction: Coover not only writes about self-conscious storytelling, he assumes that we are aware of his self-referential posture. There's no need to introduce us to the pervasive but protean "he," the author-character at the center of most of his fiction. . . .

"In Bed One Night" is a literary slapstick in which several strangers are assigned to share the same bed—social security cutbacks seem to be the

From *VLS*, no. 22 (December 1983): 4. Reprinted by permission of the author and *The Village Voice*.

problem. An old lady searches for her dentures, her one-legged brother lies at the foot of the bed, a drunken worker fucks a fat woman, and a skinny Oriental cowers, as the owner of the bed registers his shock: "wha——?! he cries out in alarm." Coover skillfully orchestrates this pandemonium in a breathless, unpunctuated style. Even when his comic technique is so emphatically in the foreground, he keeps an eye on the complexity of authorship. In his most farcical moments or his most deft and restrained moods, Coover is relentlessly energetic about one question. His fiction insists on asking where its own creativity comes from, and just as insistently answers that it exists only in the active process of writing and reading.

John O'Brien on *Spanking the Maid*

[*Spanking the Maid*] is a failed attempt to employ the methods of the *nouveau roman*; the repetitions, the variations upon images, the structural loops, the shifts in perspective, all seem wearily imitative, forced, and pretentious. Each morning a maid enters her employer's bedroom, and each morning she is spanked for her failures. . . . [There] is an implicit invitation to see how the book is constructed. . . . [However], the machinery creaks, sputters, and grinds; the tricks are telegraphed, even to the ending in which the employer and maid exchange roles. Finally, I began to suspect that some grand metaphor was rearing its ugly head. Or a fable: the man and his maid are supposed to represent the relationship between man and woman, between husband and wife, children and parents; or between artist and society, or artist and critic. No matter how well the artist does some things, so the fable might go, the critic will spank him for not doing others. . . .

From "Inventions and Conventions in the New Wave Novel," *Washington Post Book World*, 15 August 1982, 10.

Chronology

1932	Robert Coover is born 4 February in Charles City, Iowa, to Grant Marion and Maxine (Sweet) Coover.
1953	Earns B.A. from Indiana University (also attended Southern Illinois University).
1953–1957	Serves in the U.S. Navy as a lieutenant.
1959	Marries Marie del Pilar Sans-Mallafre, with whom he will have three children: Diana Nin, Sara Chapin, and Roderick Luis.
1960	"One Summer in Spain" is published in *Fiddlehead*.
1961	"Blackdamp" is published in *Noble Savage*.
1962	"The Square Shooter and the Saint" and "Dinner with the King of England" are published in *Evergreen Review*.
1963	"The Second Son" is published in *Evergreen Review*. "D.D., Baby" is published in *Cavalier*.
1965	Earns M.A. degree from University of Chicago. "The Neighbors" is published in *Argosy*.
1966	*The Origin of the Brunists* is published. Receives William Faulkner Award.
1966–1967	Teaches at Bard College.
1967	"The Mex Would Arrive at Gentry's Junction at 12:10" is published in *Evergreen Review*.
1967–1969	Teaches at University of Iowa.
1968	*The Universal Baseball Association, Inc., J. Henry Waugh, Prop.* is published. "The Cat in the Hat for President" is published in *New American Review*.
1969	*Pricksongs & Descants* is published. "Letter from Patmos" (*Quarterly Review of Literature*), "Incident in the Streets of

the City" *(Playboy)*, "That the Door Opened" *(Quarterly Review of Literature)* are published. *On a Confrontation in Iowa City,* a film, written, directed, and produced by Coover, is released. Coover receives a Rockefeller Foundation fellowship and a citation in fiction from Brandeis University. Teaches at Washington University, St. Louis.

1970   "The Reunion" and "Some Notes on Puff" published in *Iowa Review.*

1971   "The First Annual Congress of the High Church of Hard Core (Notes from the Underground)" *(Evergreen Review),* "McDuff on the Mound" *(Iowa Review)* "An Encounter" and "Debris," *(Panache), Love Scene* (play) *(New American Review),* and "The Last Quixote" (on Samuel Beckett) *(New American Review)* are published. Receives a Guggenheim Fellowship.

1972   *A Theological Position* (a collection of plays) is published. *The Water Pourer,* "Beginnings" *(Harper's)* "Lucky Pierre & the Music Lesson" *(New American Review),* "The Old Men" and "An Encounter" *(Little Magazine)* are published. American Place Theatre production of "The Kid" wins three Obie awards. Teaches at Columbia University.

1972–1973   Teaches at Princeton University.

1973   "The Dead Queen" *(Quarterly Review of Literature)* and "The Old Man" *(Panache)* are published. *Love Scene* (play) is produced in Paris.

1974   Edits *The Stonewall Book of Short Fictions. The Kid* (play) is produced in London and *Love Scene* is produced in New York. "The Public Burning of Ethel and Julius Rosenberg" *(Triquarterly)* and "Lucky Pierre and the Cunt Auction" *(Antaeus)* are published. Receives a Guggenheim Fellowship.

1975   "Whatever Happened to Gloomy Gus of the Chicago Bears" *(New American Review)* and "Lucky Pierre and the Coldwater Flat" *(Penthouse)* are published. *Rip Awake* (play) and *A Theological Position* are produced in Los Angeles.

1976   "The Fallguy's Faith" *(Triquarterly)* is published. *A Theological Position* is produced in New York. Elected to American Academy of Arts and Letters. Teaches at Virginia Military Institute.

1977   *The Public Burning* is published and nominated for a National Book Award. "The Tinkerer" *(Antaeus)*, "The Master's Voice" *(New American Review)*, and "The Convention" *(Panache)* are published.

1979   *The Hair o' the Chine* is published. "A Working Day" is published in *Iowa Review* and selected for *Best American Short Stories 1981.*

1980   "In Bed One Night" is published in *Playboy. Charlie in the House of Rue, After Lazarus,* and *A Political Fable* are published.

1980–present   Teaches at Brown University.

1981   *Spanking the Maid* is published. *Bridge Hand* (play) is produced in Providence, R.I. Teaches at Brandeis University.

1982   *The Convention* is published.

1983   *In Bed One Night & Other Brief Encounters* is published.

1984   "That F'kucken Karl Marx" is published in *fiction international.*

1985   Receives a grant from the National Endowment for the Arts.

1986   *Gerald's Party* and *Aesop's Forest* are published.

1987   *A Night at the Movies* and *Whatever Happened to Gloomy Gus of the Chicago Bears* are published. Receives a Rea Award for the Short Story from the Dungannon Foundation.

1988   "The Asian Lectures" is published in *Conjunctions.* Receives a Rhode Island Governor's Arts Award.

1989   "Lucky Pierre in the Doctor's Office" is published in *Playboy.*

1991   *Pinocchio* is published.

Bibliography

Primary Works

Collected Short Fiction

Pricksongs & Descants. New York: E. P. Dutton, 1969; New York: New American Library/Plume, 1970; London: Cape, 1971.

In Bed One Night & Other Brief Encounters. Providence, R.I.: Burning Deck Press, 1983.

A Night at the Movies or, You Must Remember This. New York: Simon & Schuster, 1987; New York: Collier Books, 1988.

Novellas

The Water Pourer. Bloomfield Hills, Mich.: Bruccoli-Clark, 1972.

Charlie in the House of Rue. Lincoln, Mass.: Penmaen, 1980.

After Lazarus. Bloomfield Hills, Mich.: Bruccoli-Clark, 1980.

A Political Fable. New York: Viking, 1980.

Spanking the Maid. Bloomfield Hills, Mich.: Bruccoli-Clark, 1981; New York: Grove Press, 1982.

Collections

The Stonewall Book of Short Fiction (ed.). Stonewall, 1974.

Uncollected Short Fiction

"Blackdamp." *Noble Savage* 4 (October 1961): 218–29.

"The Cat in the Hat for President." *New American Review* 4, 7–45. New York: New American Library, 1968.

"D.D., Baby." *Cavalier* (July 1963): 53–56, 93.

"The Dead Queen." *Quarterly Review of Literature* 8 (1973): 304–13.

"Dinner with the King of England." *Evergreen Review* 27 (November–December 1962): 110–18.

"Lucky Pierre and the Cunt Auction." *Antaeus* (Spring–Summer 1974): 13–14.

Bibliography

"Lucky Pierre and the Music Lesson." *New American Review* 14, 201–12. New York: Simon and Schuster, 1972.

"McDuff on the Mound," *Iowa Review* 2 (Fall 1971): 111–20.

"The Mex Would Arrive at Gentry's Junction at 12:10." *Evergreen Review* 47 (June 1967): 63–65, 98–102.

"The Neighbors." *Argosy* (London) (January 1965).

"The Reunion." *Iowa Review* 1 (Fall 1970): 64–69.

"The Second Son." *Evergreen Review* 27 (October–November 1963): 72–88.

"Some Notes About Puff." *Iowa Review* 1 (Winter 1970): 29–31.

"The Square Shooter and the Saint." *Evergreen Review* 25 (July–August 1962): 92–101.

"Whatever Happened to Gloomy Gus of the Chicago Bears?" *New American Review* 22 (1975): 31–111.

"The Master's Voice." *New American Review* 26 (November 1977): 361–88.

"A Working Day." *Iowa Review* 10 (Summer 1979): 1–27.

"Lucky Pierre in the Doctor's Office." *Playboy* (December 1989): 136, 212, 214, 216–17.

Secondary Works

Andersen, Richard. *Robert Coover*. Boston: Twayne, 1981.

Applefield, David. "An Interview with Robert Coover," in *Frank: An International Journal of Contemporary Writing and Art* (Paris), no. 6–7 (Winter–Spring 1987): 7–11.

Berman, Neil. "Coover's Universal Baseball Association: Play as Personalized Myth." *Modern Fiction Studies* 24, no. 2 (Summer 1978): 209–22.

Bigsby, C. W. E., and Heide Ziegler. *The Radical Imagination and the Liberal Tradition*. London: Junction Books, 1982.

Blachowicz, Camille. "Bibliography: Robert Bly and Robert Coover." *Great Lakes Review* 3 (1976): 69–73.

Cope, Jackson I. "Robert Coover's Fictions." *Iowa Review* 2 (Fall 1971): 94–110.

———. *Robert Coover's Fictions*. Baltimore: Johns Hopkins University Press, 1986.

Dillard, R. H. W. "Robert Coover." *Hollins Critic* 7, no. 2 (April 1970): 1–11.

Durand, Régis. "The Exemplary Fictions of Robert Coover." In *Les Américanistes*, ed. I. and C. Johnson. Port Washington, N.Y.: Kennikat Press, 1978.

Federman, Raymond. *Surfiction*. Chicago: Swallow Press, 1975.

Gabert, Charla. "The Metamorphosis of Charlie." *Chicago Review* 32, no. 2 (Autumn 1980): 60–64.

Gado, Frank. "Robert Coover." In *Conversations on Writers and Writing*, ed. Frank Gado, 142–59. Schenectady: Union College Press, 1973.

Gass, William H. *Fiction and the Figures of Life*. New York: Knopf, 1970; New York: Vintage, 1972.

Gordon, Lois. *Robert Coover: The Universal Fictionmaking Process*. Carbondale: Southern Illinois University Press, 1983.

Hansen, Arlen J. "The Dice of God, Einstein, Heisenberg, and Robert Coover." *Novel: A Forum on Fiction* 10 (Fall 1976): 49–58.

Harris, Charles B. "The Morning After." In *Contemporary Novelists of the Absurd*, ed. Charles B. Harris. New Haven: College and University Press, 1971.

Heckard, Margaret. "Robert Coover, Metafiction, and Freedom." *Twentieth Century Literature* 22 (1976): 219–27.

Hertzel, Leo J. "An Interview with Robert Coover." *Critique* 11 (1969): 25–29.

_____. "What's Wrong with the Christians?" *Critique* 11 (1969): 11–24.

Hume, Kathryn. "Robert Coover's Fiction: The Naked and the Mythic." *Novel: A Forum on Fiction* (Winter 1979): 127–48.

James, Caryn. [Review of *In Bed One Night & Other Brief Encounters*]. *VLS*, no. 22 (December 1983): 4.

Johnson, R. E., Jr. "Structuralism and the Reading of Contemporary Fiction." *Soundings* 58 (Fall 1975): 299–306.

Kadragic, Alma. "An Interview with Robert Coover." *Shantih* 2 (Summer 1972): 57–60.

Kennedy, Thomas E. "An Interview with Robert Coover." *AWP Chronicle* (February 1991): 11–12.

Kissel, Susan. "The Contemporary Artist and His Audience in the Short Stories of Robert Coover." *Studies in Short Fiction* 16, no. 1 (Winter 1979): 52–54.

Klinkowitz, Jerome. *Literary Disruptions: The Making of a Post-Contemporary Fiction*. Urbana: University of Illinois Press, 1975.

McCaffery, Larry. "Donald Barthelme, Robert Coover, William H. Gass: Three Checklists." *Bulletin of Bibliography* 31 (July–September 1974): 101–6.

_____. "Robert Coover." In *The Dictionary of Literary Biography*, vol. 2., ed. J. Helterman and R. Layman, 106–21. Detroit: Bruccoli-Clark/Gale Research, 1978.

_____. "The Magic of Fiction-Making." *Fiction International* 4–5 (Winter 1975): 147–53.

_____. "An Interview with Robert Coover." In *Anything Can Happen: Interviews with Contemporary American Novelists*, ed. Tom LeClair and Larry McCaffery, 63–78. Urbana, Ill.: University of Illinois Press, 1983.

Pearse, James A. "Beyond the Narrational Frame: Interpretation and Metafiction." *Quarterly Review of Speech* 66 (February 1980): 73–84.

Schmitz, Neil. "A Prisoner of Words." *Partisan Review* 40 (Winter 1973): 131–35.

_____. "Robert Coover and the Hazards of Metafiction." *Novel: A Forum on Fiction* 7 (Spring 1974): 210–19.

Bibliography

Scholes, Robert. *Fabulation and Metafiction*. Urbana: University of Illinois Press, 1979.

Schultz, Max F. "Politics of Parody." In *Black Humor Fiction of the Sixties*, ed. Max F. Schultz. Athens: Ohio University Press, 1973.

Shelton, Frank. "Humor and Balance in Coover's *The Universal Baseball Association*." *Critique* 5 (August 1975): 78–90.

Wineapple, Brenda. "Robert Coover's Playing Fields." *Iowa Review* 10 (1979): 66–74.

Woolf, Geoffrey. "An American Epic." *New Times* 9 (August 1977): 48–57.

Zavarzaden, Mas'ud. *The Mythopoeic Reality*. Urbana: University of Illinois Press, 1976.

Zonderman, Jon. [Review of *Charlie in the House of Rue*]. *American Book Review* 4, no. 2 (January–February 1982): 24.

Index

American Book Review, 122
American studies, 122
Andersen, Richard
   Robert Coover, xi, 18, 29, 35, 36, 38,
     42, 45, 59, 62, 66, 71
Anti-illusion, 23
Apocalypse, 111
Applefield, David, 112–18
Aristotle, 117
Astaire, Fred, 87
Asturias, 116
Auster, Paul
   New York Trilogy, 10

Barth, John, 5, 76, 116, 121, 130
   Lost in the Funhouse, 5, 76
Bartheleme, Donald, 5, 6, 119, 120,
    121, 130
   *Unspeakable Practices, Unnatural
    Acts*, 5
Barthelme, Frederick, 6
Beckett, Samuel, 6, 47, 100, 130,
    134, 142
Bettelheim, Bruno
   The Uses of Enchantment, 8, 13, 14,
    15, 28, 30
Bible, 7, 8. *See also* "The Brother" and
   "J's Marriage"
   Genesis, 36, 37
   John, 77, 130
   Sodom and Gomorrah, 36, 72
Blixen, Karen, 88
Borges, Jorges Luis, 66, 106, 116, 130
Breslin, Jimmy, 4, 5
Burroughs, William, 62, 116

Caiaphas, 77
Calvino, Italo, 100, 105, 116, 120, 121

Capote, Truman, 3, 4, 5
   In Cold Blood, 3
Carroll, Lewis, 25
Carter, Angela, 100
Carver, Raymond, 6, 9, 112, 121
Casablanca, 75, 87, 88
Cervantes, 32, 33, 36, 48, 130
Chandler, Raymond, 75
Chaplin, Charlie, 83–84, 134–39
Chaucer, 122
   Wife of Bath, 12
Chekhov, Anton, 7
Christ, 78
Christianity, 111, 113, 117
Cold war, 100
Coleridge, Samuel Taylor, 33, 89
Collective unconscious, 4
Colorado Review, 6
Computers, 115
Cool Hand Luke, 26
Coover, Robert, works
   Aesop's Forest, 143
   After Lazarus, 76–79, 88, 111, 143
   "The Babysitter," 8, 62–64, 128
   "Beginnings," 71–72, 134, 139
   "Blackdamp," 141
   Bridge Hand, 143
   "The Brother," 8, 36–38, 42–43,
    79, 132
   "Cartoon," 85–86, 114
   "The Cat in the Hat for President,"
    111, 141
   Charlie in the House of Rue, 83–84,
    85, 111, 127, 134–39, 143
   "The Convention," 70–71
   "D. D., Baby, 141
   "The Dead Queen," 142
   "The Debris," 68, 142
   "Dinner with the King of
    England," 141

Coover, Robert, works, *cont.*
"The Door: A Prologue of Sorts," 8, 12–15, 27, 30, 31, 132
"The Elevator," 8, 46–50, 62, 106, 128
"An Encounter," 70, 139, 142
"The Fallguy's Faith," 69–70, 143
"The First Annual Congress of the High Church of Hard Core," 142
Gerald's Party, 11, 114, 118, 143
"Getting to Wichita," 69
"Gilda's Dream," 81–82
"The Gingerbread House," 8, 26–32, 132
Hair o' the Chine, 111, 143
"The Hat Act," 64–67, 79, 129, 131, 132, 133, 134
"In a Train Station," 38–39
"In Bed One Night," 69, 139, 143
In Bed One Night & Other Brief Encounters, xi, 68–72, 120, 127, 139–40, 143
"Incident in the Streets of the City," 142
"Inside the Frame," 82
"Intermission," 84–85
"J's Marriage," 8, 40–44, 79, 132
The Kid, 104, 105, 142
"Klee Dead," 39–40, 133
"Lap Dissolves," 82–83
"The Last Quixote," 142
"The Leper's Helix, 59–60, 79
"Letter from Patmos," 141
Love Scene, 104, 142
Lucky Pierre stories, xii, 142, 143
"McDuff on the Mound," 142
"The Magic Poker," 15–24, 62, 71, 72
"The Marker," 34–36
"The Mex Would Arrive at Gentry's Junction at 12:10." *See* "Shootout at Gentry's Junction"
"Milford Junction, 1939: A Brief Encounter," 86–87
"The Milkmaid of Salmaniego," 57–59

"Morris in Chains," 24–26, 130
"The Neighbors," 141
A Night at the Movies, xi, 10, 73–90, 127, 143
"The Old Man," 68–69, 139
On a Confrontation in Iowa City, 142
"One Summer in Spain," 141
The Origin of the Brunists, 11, 103, 105, 106, 141
"Panel Game," 33–34, 106
"A Pedestrian Accident," 60–62
"The Phantom of the Movie Palace," 34, 73–76, 78
Pinocchio, 11, 142
A Political Fable, 111, 143
Pricksongs & Descants, xi, 3, 5, 7, 8, 10, 12–67, 72, 91, 120, 127, 128–31, 133–34, 137
"Prologue," 32–33
The Public Burning, 8, 11, 97, 103, 107, 108, 109, 110, 111, 120, 143
"The Public Burning of Ethel and Julius Rosenberg," 142
"Quenby and Ola, Swede and Carl," 52–55
"The Reunion," 142
Rip Awake, 105
"The Romance of the Thin Man and the Fat Lady," 50–52, 132
"Scene for Winter," 55–57, 76
"The Second Son," 141
"Selected Short Subjects," 81–83
"The Sentient Lens," 32, 55–62, 76
"Seven Exemplary Fictions," 32–46, 106
"Shootout at Gentry's Junction," 79–81, 82, 93, 141
"Some Notes on Puff," 142
Spanking the Maid, 10, 120, 127, 140, 143
"The Square Shooter and the Saint," 141
"That F'kucken Karl Marx," 143
"That the Door Opened," 142
A Theological Position, 105, 142
"The Tinkerer," 69
"Top Hat," 87

The Universal Baseball Association,
    11, 121, 141
The Water Pourer, 142
"The Wayfarer," 44–46
*Whatever Happened to Gloomy Gus
    of the Chicago Bears?* 108, 120,
    142, 143
"A Working Day," 143
"You Must Remember This," 87–89
Cope, Jackson I.
    Robert Coover's Fictions, xi, 59, 73,
        76, 78, 82, 85, 87, 91
Cortazar, Julio, 116
Costello, Mark, 121
Coward, Noel
    Brief Encounter, 86–87
Crowley, Aleister, 65
Cubism, 9, 71

Dillard, R. H. W., 65–66
Disney, Walt, 12, 32
Dostoevski, Fyodor, 116
Dubus, Andre, 6
Durkheim, Emile, 116
Dylan, Bob, 26

Edson, Russell, 68
Eisenhower, Dwight D., 107
Eliot, T. S., 84
    Prufrock, 44
Elkin, Stanley, 116, 122

Fabulism, 6
Fairy tales, 7, 8, 12
    "Beauty and the Beast," 12
    "Hansel and Gretel," 27, 31, 32,
        128, 120
    "Jack and the Beanstalk," 12–15
    "Little Red Riding Hood," 12–15,
        19, 24, 30
Fanny Hill, 12
Farce, 13, 114
Faulkner, William, 9, 116
FBI, 107

Fiction and the Figures of Life. See
    Gass, William H.
Fiction Collective, 98, 99
Fitzgerald, F. Scott, 9
Flaubert, Gustav, 116
Forster, E. M., 16, 49, 121
Frank: An International Journal, 6, 112
Freud, Sigmund, 116
Fuentes, Carlos, 116

Gabert, Charla, 127, 135–39
Gardner, John, 102
Gass, William H.
    Fiction and the Figures of Life, 4, 16,
        18, 86, 127, 128–31
Gilmore, Gary, 4
Gogol, Nikolay
    "The Nose," 7
Gordon, Lois
    *Robert Coover: The Univerasl
        Fiction-Making Process,* xi, 21, 35,
        38, 45, 49, 59, 78, 92
Gorey, Edward, 121
Gould, Chester, 61
Granta, 6, 121
Grass, Gunther, 100, 116
Grimm, Jacob and Wilhelm, 3, 8, 12,
    27, 29. *See also* Fairy tales

Hamill, Pete, 4
Hawkes, John, 98, 116
Hayworth, Rita, 81
Helms, Jesse, 68, 97
Helzapoppin, 61
Hemingway, Ernest, 9, 116
High Noon, 79
Homer, 4
Hoover, J. Edgar, 107
Hope, Bob, 75
Houseman, A. E., 39

James, Caryn, 127
James, Henry, 42, 44
    "The Beast in the Jungle," 44

Index

Jameson, Frederick, 133
Jaspers, Karl, 36
"John Henry," 26
Johnson, Chic, 61
Journalism, 3, 4, 5, 8, 101
Joyce, James, 6, 65, 92n17
    Bloom, Leopold, 41
    Bloom, Molly, 12, 41
Jung, Carl, 81, 93, 122

Kafka, Franz, 6, 41, 66, 116, 138
Kant, Immanuel, 116
Kennedy, Thomas E., 119–23
Kent State, 113
Kesey, Ken, 24, 26
    One Flew Over the Cuckoo's Nest, 24
Kierkegard, Soren, 77, 116
Kissel, Susan, 127, 132–33

Levy, Eliphas, 65

McCaffery, Larry, 97, 98–111
McPherson, James Alan, 121
Magic, 16, 89, 114. See also "The Hat Act"
Mailer, Norman, 3, 4, 88
    Armies of the Night, 4
    Miami and the Siege of Chicago, 4
    The Executioner's Song, 4, 5, 88
Ma Kettle, 12
Malamud, Bernard
    "The Jewbird,", 5
    Pictures of Fidelman, 5
Manners, 19
Mason, Bobbie Anne, 6, 121–22
Melville, Herman, 66, 116
Metafiction, 5, 6, 8, 9, 13, 24, 32, 36, 68, 71, 127, 133. See also Self-reflexive action
Miller, Henry, 88, 116
Millman, Lawrence, 8
Milton, John, 39
Mimeses, 7
Minimalism, 6, 116
Modernism, 6, 44

Moore, Marianne, 60
Moral fiction, 102

Nabokov, Vladimir, 17, 66, 116, 121
National Endowment for the Arts, 68, 97
Nazism, 113
Newton, 117
New World, 24, 33, 36, 66, 67
Nixon, Richard M., 8, 36–38, 42–43, 79, 132
Norton Anthology of Short Fiction, 121
Nouveau roman, 116, 140

Oates, Joyce Carol, 127, 131–32
O'Brien, John, 127, 140
O'Connor, Frank, 21
Olsen, Ole, 61
Orwell, George, 36

Pan, 24
Percy, Walker, 117, 118
Perrault, Charles, 12, 13
Plato, 117
Playboy, xii, 69
Poe, Edgar Allen
    "Ligeia," 66
    "The Predicament," 61
Politicians, 115
Pornography, 21
Postmodernism, 6, 7, 8, 10, 119
Pynchon, Thomas, 6, 116
    Vineland, 6

Reagan, Ronald, 115
Realism, 3–10, 12, 13, 112, 122
Reality, 3–5, 9–12, 14, 31, 88, 89
Rosenberg, Julius and Ethel, 110
Rosset, Barney, 110

Sappho, 117
Schmitz, Neil, 13, 127, 133–34
Sexual revolution, 114
Scholes, Robert, 98

152

Self-reflexive action, 102. *See also*
    Metafiction
Shakespeare, William
    A Midnight Summer's Dream, 17,
      24, 33
    Much Ado about Nothing, 34
    The Tempest, Caliban, Prospero, 16,
      22, 24
Shiva, 17
Slapstick, 13, 33, 61, 83
Solotaroff, Ted, 110
Southern, Terry
    Candy, 85
Spielberg, Steven
    Raiders of the Lost Arc, 85
    Who Killed Roger Rabbit? 12, 85
Stevens, Wallace
    "Peter Quince at the Clavier,"
      17, 78
Streep, Meryl, 88
Surrealism, 6, 8

Thompson, Hunter S., 4
A Thousand Clowns, 26
Twain, Mark, 26

Updike, John
    Couples, 8
U.S. Supreme Court, 21

Valery, Paul, 12
Vonnegut, Kurt
    Cat's Cradle, 26

Weaver, Gordon
    "The Parts of Speech," 66
West, Nathaniel, 116
Wolfe, Tobias, 6
Wolfe, Tom, 4, 5
    Bonfire of the Vanities, 4
Wordsworth, William, 59
Writing programs, 112

Yeats, W. B., 65, 66
Yuppies, 113

Zola, Emile, 4
Zonderman, 127, 134–35

The Author

Thomas E. Kennedy's books include a novel, *Crossing Borders;* an essay collection, *The American Short Story Today;* and *Andre Dubus: A Study of the Short Fiction.* His fiction and nonfiction have appeared in some 80 North American and European journals and anthologies, and he is a recipient of the Pushcart Prize (1990–91). Thomas Kennedy has an M.F.A. from Vermont College of Norwich University and a Ph.D. in the contemporary American short story from Copenhagen University. He has taught at Vermont College, the European Division of the University of Maryland, the Emerson College International Writing Workshop in the Netherlands, and the Women's Institute for Continuing Education in Paris. He and his wife, Monique, a physician and translator, have collaborated on translations of Danish prose and poetry.

The Editor

General editor Gordon Weaver earned his B.A. in English at the University of Wisconsin-Milwaukee in 1961; his M.A. in English at the University of Illinois, where he studied as a Woodrow Wilson Fellow, in 1962; and his Ph.D. in English and creative writing at the University of Denver in 1970. His novels include *Count a Lonely Cadence, Give Him a Stone, Circling Byzantium,* and *The Eight Corners of the World.* Many of his short stories are collected in *The Entombed Man of Thule, Such Waltzing Was Not Easy, Getting Serious, Morality Play, A World Quite Round,* and *Men Who Would Be Good.* He edited *The American Short Story, 1945–1980: A Critical History,* and is currently editor of *Cimarron Review.* He is professor of English at Oklahoma State University and serves as an adjunct member of the faculty of the Vermont College Master of Fine Arts in Writing Program.